DURYODHAN*IZATION*

DURYODHAN*IZATION*

ARE VILLAINS BORN, MADE, OR MADE UP?

NISHANT UPPAL

PENGUIN
BUSINESS

An imprint of Penguin Random House

PENGUIN BUSINESS

USA | Canada | UK | Ireland | Australia
New Zealand | India | South Africa | China | Singapore

Portfolio is part of the Penguin Random House group of companies
whose addresses can be found at global.penguinrandomhouse.com

Published by Penguin Random House India Pvt. Ltd
4th Floor, Capital Tower 1, MG Road,
Gurugram 122 002, Haryana, India

Penguin
Random House
India

First published in Portfolio by Penguin Random House India 2018
This edition published in Penguin Business by Penguin Random House India 2024

ISBN 9780670090334

Typeset in PalmSprings by Manipal Digital Systems, Manipal
Printed at Replika Press Pvt. Ltd, India

www.penguin.co.in

MIX
Paper from
responsible sources
FSC® C016779

This is a legitimate digitally printed version of the book and therefore might not
have certain extra finishing on the cover.

To
Sukhdeep (Papa), Vihaan and Kabir (sons)

CONTENTS

PREFACE

A reader quick, keen and leery
Did wonder, ponder and query
When results clean and tight
Fit predictions just right
If the data preceded the theory

—*Anonymous*

It gives me immense pleasure to introduce this book, *Duryodhanization*, to my esteemed readers. This book attempts to explain the process involved in the making of a villain. It uses Duryodhana, a popular villain from the epic Mahabharata, as the central character to understand the process. Thus, the title: Duryodhanization. Although there are several famous villains in the world, in literature, and in the Mahabharata itself, the character of Duryodhana is especially intriguing. Thousands of versions of the Mahabharata, as well as books focusing on some of its characters, have been written over the centuries. None of them show Duryodhana in a positive light. The Bhagavad Gita from the Mahabharata, clearly states that every individual has *daivi* (good) and *asuri* (bad) qualities. However, there is nothing positive about Duryodhana's character in the Mahabharata. And this epic is considered to be the longest poem ever written, with over two lakh lines and eighteen lakh words. This is surprising and worth exploring further.

Following is a brief, chapter-wise description of the book. This is for the reader to understand the premise, purpose and conception of the book.

Chapter one introduces the concept of the making of a villain. I use multiple theoretical lenses to decipher whether villains are born, nurtured or merely made up. I use theories from a range of academic disciplines, such as psychology, genetic sciences, sociology, economics, etymology, history and management, to get a clearer understanding of the central concept of the book. Seminal research work, historical and modern, has been considered while exploring the process of Duryodhanization.

Chapter two defines some commonly acknowledged psychological dispositions. These include Machiavellianism narcissism, neuroticism, psychopathy and sadism, which make a villain a negative character or person. It also hypothesizes that these traits can be genetically transmitted and are contagious. I again use theories from various disciplines to support my arguments.

In chapter three we explore our central character, Duryodhana. I use various scientifically valid methodologies to analyse his actions as presented in the Mahabharata. I further map those actions along with the five negative dispositions described in the previous chapter.

Sub-sections one, two and three in this chapter look at Duryodhana's family tree, examining the possibilities of genetic transmission of the five negative dispositions into Duryodhana. For this, I analyse the actions of Duryodhana's ancestors and map them along the negative dispositions mentioned above. And here, we find some remarkable linkages between the two. It clearly establishes how genetics influenced Duryodhana's behaviour throughout his life.

While it is clear that genetics played a significant role in determining Duryodhana's character, there are other possible explanations. In chapter four, I examine the behaviour of other important characters in the Mahabharata, such as the Pandava brothers and Draupadi. I list several actions of the Pandavas that are very similar to Duryodhana's. However, they are treated differently in the epic, and thereafter by other readers and writers. While it seems unfair, the various explanations and justifications of the war between good and evil are what make the epic so interesting.

Chapter five explores the possibilities of generalizing of the concept of Duryodhanization. I choose characters, living and dead, and juxtapose them with the findings of the book. I have chosen these characters with utmost care to avoid hurting the sentiments of any community.

Finally, in the last chapter I conclude my theories and arguments. Only here do I allow my personal views on the subject to come forth.

I believe this book will appeal to the curiosity of those who wish to scientifically understand the characterization of heroes or villains, be it in mythology, history, behavioural sciences, or real life. It also has teachings for businesses, academia and policy organizations, as the book presents an unusual method of character assessment. I hope it will provide stimulus for further research and literature.

Lastly, I would like to acknowledge my peers and editors, especially Radhika and Indrani who reviewed and worked tirelessly towards the current edition. I would like to acknowledge my research associate, Ananya, for her inputs. I am thankful to my friends—Badri, Neha, Negi, and Gautam.

I am grateful to my mom, Shivani Uppal, who continuously encouraged me to take up this project. I am also thankful to Deepti, my beloved wife, for her immense support. I am grateful to various members of IIM Lucknow, especially Professor Ajit Prasad who provided motivation to complete the work. Without their contributions this project would not have been possible.

Introduction

Son: 'Do ostriches bury their heads in the sand when they're scared or threatened?'

Father: 'No, it's an optical illusion! Ostriches are the largest living birds, but their heads are pretty small. If you see them picking at the ground from a distance, it may look like their heads are buried in the ground. Nonetheless, they do dig holes in the dirt to use as nests for their eggs. Several times a day, the bird puts her head in the hole and turns the eggs. So it really does look like the birds are burying their heads in the sand!'

Son: 'Oh! This means the ostrich creates an optical illusion, possibly intentionally, that makes the viewer seem as if it is hiding its head in the sand. Wow, that's an ostrich paradox!'

According to the Oxford English Dictionary, a character is defined as villainous if his or her actions or motives are considered evil towards other individuals, nations, societies, environments or the universe as a whole. The essence of this book lies in the etymological and colloquial development and popular establishment of this definition.

Although today the term villain is used only in a pejorative sense, originally it defined entirely different phenomena and characters. The etymological development of the term villain follows this order: *villa-villanus-vilain* (or *vilein*)-villain. The first two terms of the sequence *villa* and *villanus* descend from Latin, and mean country mansion and farmland bound to the soil of that mansion, respectively. Subsequently, the French term *vilain* refers to a person of less-knightly attributes. One who was usually employed as a peasant, slave or farm hand.

In the Middle Ages, the French aristocracy was mostly dominated by men. In order to safeguard and monopolize their women, they propagated the physically laborious vilains as impolite and unchivalrous. They used various vehicles such as literature and executive gatherings to alter the meaning. The etymological development or deterioration of the term villain continued as various other pejorative meanings, such as despicable, shameful, morally corrupt, knave, scoundrel, boor and, finally, criminal, were added to it.

The process of degradation of a phenomenon is not unique to the science of etymology.[1] Scholars of sociology and cultural anthropology have acknowledged such degradations at a macro social level. For example, the degradation of the Vaishyas and the Shudras through the complex process of verticalization of the Indian caste system through the Middle Ages and thereafter. In a study of the Hindu varna system, Kavoori (2002) highlighted that over 700 years ago, a gradual deterioration came about in the status of the Vaishyas and the Shudras. These communities lost their equal status and acquired lower ranks than the other two varnas, the Brahmana and the Kshatriya. The study suggests that the varna system was originally horizontal in nature with a scientific division of labour and professions. It is believed that the advent of the Aryans in India and their influence over scholarly works and literature, such as the Manusmriti, is mainly responsible for the verticalization of the varna system. Manusmriti, a book that has been condemned for centuries, regulated the ideals of administration, social behaviour and the canons of justice. This established the supremacy of the Brahmanas and the Kshatriyas over the Vaishyas and the Shudras. Gandhi sincerely hated the practice of untouchability, the worst form of vertical varna system. He supported the conventional varna system, saying that, 'some (people) believe that I (Gandhi) am destroying varna ashrama. On the contrary I believe that I am trying to cleanse it of impurities and so reveal its true form' (*Collected Works*, 1921, vol. 20).

Some developed countries use the same mechanism of systematic defamation and degradation while viewing less-developed nations. Only the vehicles of defamation and degradation may differ contextually. Cinema is among the most dramatic vehicles popularly used for this purpose. Lee (2007) undertook a study highlighting the brutal use of cinema, specifically in James Bond 007 movies to illustrate the dark side of North Korea. She analysed a total of fifteen newspaper articles about the movie *007 Die Another Day*. They included Western (e.g. *New York Times*, *Chicago Tribune*, and *Los Angeles Times*), and Eastern publications (e.g. *Korean Herald*, *Good Day News*, and *Metro*). These articles were published between December 2002 and February 2003. The data of the study showed how the movie, with a total revenue of $432 million and a worldwide viewership, contributed to building a maligned image of a country. Some articles highlighted the fact that the movie put North Korea in 'the axis of evil' and was a 'deliberate and premeditated act of mocking at and insulting the

Korean nation'. In reaction to this, the Korean nationals boycotted the movie due to its 'distorted depiction of North Korea'. A limited boycott stood against a worldwide acceptance of the movie. Dodds (2005) asserted that some viewers found the movie very realistic and felt threatened by the North Korean villain in the film and thereafter in reality. It is evident that motion pictures, such as the James Bond 007 series, propagate American hegemony by popularizing different negative aspects of the international environment (Shin and Namkung, 2008).

There are several other vehicles that are used, consciously or unconsciously, with the purpose of building a bleak image of foreign nations. The notorious American-Iraq war was based solely on this image. It is now public information that there were no weapons of mass destruction in Iraq's possession, which was the primary cause behind America's attack on Iraq. Several scholars, such as Kull and associates (2003) and Cirincione and associates (2004), now postulate that the reason for the failure of intelligence was more deliberate and less of a casual mistake. Kull et al. (2003) write the following in their article:

> From the outset, the Bush administration was faced with unique challenges in its efforts to legitimate its decision to go to war. Because the war was not prompted by an overt act against the United States or its interests, and was not approved by UN Security Council, the Bush administration argued that the war was necessary on the basis of a potential threat. Because the evidence for this threat was not fully manifest, the Bush administration led the public to believe that Iraq was developing weapons of mass destruction (WMD) and providing substantial support to the al-Qaeda terrorist groups.

Robert Jervis (2010) in his article 'Why Intelligence Fails: Lessons from the Iranian Revolution and the Iraq War' talks about the precursor to a substandard decision, such as the American attack on Iraq, and the subsequent use of media to build a negative image of the country as justification for faulty actions. He says that this sometimes results from inefficient intelligence. It can be argued that critical deficiencies in intelligence occur because of analytical failure. Analysts either fail to articulate their assumptions, or don't subject these assumptions to appropriate scrutiny, or consider rival hypotheses based on evidence, test arguments by offering predictions, consider negative and positive evidence when evaluating assertions and seek information that might disconfirm their existing point of view. Once the intelligence agencies have confirmed a hypothesis, such as the existence of weapons of mass destruction in Iraq, decision makers are compelled to react, even in the face of extremely fallible consensus.

Similarly, sometimes a whole era carries a negative image. Even though the process and factors behind the negative image may differ, for example, the Dark Ages of Europe. The term 'Dark Ages' refers to the time in Europe between the fall of Rome in 476 CE and the beginning of the Renaissance in the fourteenth century. Historians consider it to be a period of sharp demographic, intellectual and economic decline. But were the Dark Ages completely dark? Or was the idea of darkness a deliberately built perception?

Some historians have established signs of immense light during the Dark Ages. These signs are scarce but significant. In his book *European Literature and the Latin Middle Ages*, Ernst Robert Curtius presents strong evidence of significant improvements seen during the Dark Ages. Dante Alighieri (1265–1312), the famous literary icon, was born during this time. He contributed immensely to literature with his two famous compositions, *Comedia* and *Boccaccio*. Dante also challenged the use of Latin in literature for it limited its access to affluent and educated audiences only. He later went on to promote the use of the vernacular in literature. Jean Gimpel in his book *The Medieval Machine: The Industrial Revolution of the Middle Ages*, highlights the environmental concerns of industries during that period and the subsequent use of alternative energy sources such as wind and water. There are several other intellectual accomplishments and scientific discoveries that took place during the Dark Ages. These have been ignored or overpowered by scholarly contributions that selectively highlight the achievements of the eras pre and post Dark Ages.

The four examples above—the term villain, the Indian caste system, national image and a historical period—differ in their parameters for analysis. Yet they all suffered conscious and systematic degradation of meaning and image in some aspects. Villain is a word that has suffered etymological deterioration. The Vaishyas and the Shudras in the Indian caste system systematically lost their equal stature to the Brahman and the Kshatriya classes. Similarly, while some countries such as Iraq or North Korea were subject to deliberate attempts of defamation by developed nations, the bright sides of the Dark Ages in Europe remain unacknowledged.

Parochialism, ethnocentrism and orientalism are well-established theories that may explain the process of systematic deterioration in various phenomena. All three theories primarily originate from the concept of 'deliberate ignorance of truth'. Though these theories differ in their scope, they beautifully unearth the process by which deteriorated images turn into knowledge and subsequently into truth.

Parochialism is based on ignorance of others' ways. Parochialism in knowledge occurs when scholars develop theories within a limited context and, consciously or unconsciously, ignore other models, research and values. Boyacigiller and Adler (1991) postulated three kinds of knowledge-based parochialism: contextual, quantitative and qualitative. Following is the process of contextual parochialism (American in this case) in the words of Boyacigiller and Adler:

> First, scholars produce and disseminate the majority of organizational science research within the United States. Second, the scope and primary orientation of most theories is American; however, such theories are presented as if they were universally applicable. For example, researchers conduct studies on the job satisfaction of American men and yet use the results to develop and substantiate overall theories on job satisfaction. A few scholars then test these US job satisfaction theories to see if they apply abroad.

Because the dominant nationality of various theories is American, it always leads to and constructs knowledge domains. For example, researchers from other countries are bound to refer to the theories published in top American journals. The essence of scholarly innovation lies in the falsification[2] of existing theories. Illogical as it seems, internationalized theories are also now a subdivision of domestic US knowledge. They are merely posed as having a 'universal perspective'.

Qualitative parochialism emerges from issues associated with the 'difficulties of breaking the American-based, logical empiricist mold'. Boyacigiller and Adler (1991) accurately say:

Given that few international articles have been published and that articles published in foreign journals are of suspect quality by many American editorial boards, international researchers are hard pressed to 'ritualistically affirm group membership'. That is, to cite a sufficient number of relevant articles published in leading American journals to pass the test of 'building on prior research'.

Therefore, research methods are painfully driving knowledge production rather than addressing the problems and needs of managers, policymakers and students.

Further, qualitative parochialism refers to the fact that 'science has reflected primarily the American cultural values of rationality and free will'. Qualitative parochialism occurs when theories are either not based on universal values or when those values do not have an impact on the overall social behaviour of individuals. For example, Hofstede (1981, 32) found remarkable differences in focus according to the particular researcher's background. According to Jones and Nisbett (1971), qualitative parochialism is a natural outcome of an attribution error. They quote:

> . . . the fundamental attribution error posits that individuals are prone to view the behavior of others as determined by their individual characteristics and motivations rather than by characteristics of the environment.

Therefore, scholars subconsciously underestimate the extent to which their perceptions, interpretations and knowledge building are influenced by their cultural environment rather than the environment of the subject they are studying.

Another theory describing the systematic deterioration of an image is ethnocentrism. Ethnocentrism was introduced to sociological literature nearly a century ago and is defined as:

> . . . the view of things in which one's own group is the center of everything, and all others are scaled and rated with reference to it . . . Each group nourishes its own pride and vanity, boasts itself superior, exalts its own divinities and looks with contempt on outsiders (Sumner 1906, 13).

Ethnocentrism is not confined only to tribes and nations. It reveals itself in all kinds of social groups—developing into family pride, sectionalism, religious prejudice, racial discrimination and patriotism. It is argued that ethnocentrism is a part of human nature. According to Levine and Campbell (1972), properties of ethnocentrism include the tendency (1) to distinguish between various groups; (2) to perceive events in terms of the group's own interests (economical, political, and social); (3) to see one's own group as the centre of the universe and to regard its way of life as superior to all others; (4) to be suspicious of and have disdain towards other groups; (5) to view one's own group as superior, strong and honest; (6) and to see other groups as inferior, weak and dishonest troublemakers.

The final theoretical background that describes and analyses deliberate deterioration of a subject's image is orientalism. In one of the most influential academic works of the twentieth century, Edward Said (1978) coined the term orientalism. He used it to refer to a style of thought based upon an ontological and epistemological distinction made between the 'orient' and the 'occident'. In the words of Said:

... a very large mass of writers, among whom are poets, novelists, philosophers, political theorists, economists and imperial administrators, have accepted the basic distinction between East and West as the starting point for elaborate theories, epics, novels, social descriptions and political accounts concerning the Orient, its people, customs, 'mind', destiny and so on.

. . . Orientalism can be discussed and analyzed as the corporate institution for dealing with the Orient—dealing with it by making statements about it, authorizing views of it, describing it, by teaching it settling it, ruling over it: in short, Orientalism as a Western style for dominating restructuring, and having authority over the Orient.

And finally, orientalism is:

. . . systematic discipline by which European culture was able to manage—and even produce—the Orient politically, sociologically, militarily, ideologically, scientifically and imaginatively during the post-Enlightenment period.

Orientalism occurs in phases. Phase one is the systematic examination and theorizing of a subject. The definition and characteristics attributed to the subject are not necessarily present in the subject. They are created by the imaginations, perceptions, prejudices and ideologies of influential scholars engaged in the examination of that subject. In the second phase, the process of orientalism is reinforced by multiple studies. These are conducted by disciples and scholars from various scientific disciplines, who are interested in understanding the subject by referring to the first phase of orientalism. In the third phase, the definition of the subject becomes substantially legitimized. An authority is bestowed on to the definition, initiated primarily on imagination. And finally, in the fourth stage, the originality of the subject is lost or becomes significantly limited. Thus, according to Said, orientalism is defined as the systematic creation and manipulation of knowledge by the 'occident' about the 'orient'.

We have discussed above a systematic and intellectual degradation in the meaning or status of macro-level phenomena such as caste, nation or historical periods. However, individuals are also subject to such scholarly treatments.

There are several reasons to believe in the possibility of significant differences in reality and the popular knowledge or image of an individual. To put it simply, according to different scholars of different times, the Earth was believed to be of different shapes—ranging from flat to oval, to finally, as we now know—partially round.

Scholars in the field of personality and individual differences suggest that no subject is completely negative or positive in its effects over other subjects. They suggest that at low to moderate levels, some positive characteristics associated with an individual may add to positive inferences by others. However, the same characteristics may be viewed by others as highly counterproductive. For example, honesty is a highly acceptable and preferred trait in an individual. But it is not always productive or beneficial. Suppose a compulsive psychopath rapist is chasing a girl who is hidden in a stack of wood. He asks an onlooker about the girl's whereabouts. Honesty from that onlooker is absolutely undesirable. The same concept may apply to negative characteristics. For example, excessive narcissism as a personality trait is generally associated with negative behavioural outcomes such as self-centeredness, arrogance, manipulation and exploitation. However, low to moderate levels may be considered beneficial due to other associated dimensions such as charisma, fearlessness and boldness.

Scholars (Grant and Schwartz, 2011; Pierce and Aguinis, 2013) in the field of personality and individual differences refer to such paradoxical outcomes as TMGT (too-much-of-a-good-thing) effects. TMGT refers to an apparent contradiction where the presence of a characteristic in an individual at low or high levels may have paradoxical effects on certain behavioural outcomes. Therefore, a person with negative characteristics may also exhibit positive behaviours in certain contexts, though these are scarcely highlighted.

Another issue associated with the negative image of an individual lies in the theories of personality development. Researchers in the field of developmental psychology have long debated whether a person is born with a personality attribute or develops with various experiences—the nurture vs nature theory. Behaviour-genetic models (nature) focus on the degree of biological relatedness and specific markers of genetically linked characteristics between individuals. The developmental models (nurture) primarily assess variations in personality according to differences in the environment. Further, a more contemporary interactionist approach studies the interplay between genetic and environmental factors. The interactionist approach measures whether individuals with shared genetics respond differently to similar environmental conditions. The personality dispositions observed in an individual may be an outcome of either the genetic composition, the environmental surroundings or an interplay between the genes and the environment. Thus, a critical examination becomes essential to hold the individual responsible for his or her negative actions.

Considerable research has focused on explaining human behaviour. Research on genetics has built a strong case for the importance of genetic factors in many complex behavioural disorders, and also in the domains of psychopathology, personality, cognitive abilities and overall human behaviour. In particular, the role of familial influences on human behaviour has been studied extensively. Rhee and Waldman (2002) undertook a meta-study and found significant effects of dysfunctional familial influences—such as psychopathology in the parents, coercive parenting styles, physical abuse and family conflict—on human behaviour.

In addition, several statistical models have been validated to assess the effects of genetics on human behaviour. Jinks and Fulker (1970) highlighted the usefulness of several of these techniques. According to them:

> There are currently three alternative approaches to the genetical analysis of human twin and familial data. There is the classical approach. This involves correlations between relatives and the culmination of various estimated ratios describing the relative importance of genetic and environmental influences on trait variation. This approach leads to ratios such as the // of Holzinger (1929), the E of Neel and Schull (1954) and the HR of Nichols (1965). Each of these measures an aspect of the relative importance of heredity and environment. There is the more systematic and comprehensive approach of the Multiple Abstract Variance Analysis (MAVA) developed by Cattell (1960, 1965). This leads to the estimation of nature: nurture ratios as well as an assessment of the importance of the correlation between genetic and environmental influences within family and within culture.

This approach is based on the comparison of within and between-family variances of full and half-sib families, as well as monozygotic and dizygotic twins. Finally there is the biometrical, genetical approach that was initiated by Fisher (1918) and applied by Mather (1949). It includes the first two approaches as special cases. And then attempts to go beyond them to an assessment of the kind of gene action and mating system operating in the population.

Further, the association between troubled parental marriage and children's psychiatric disturbance is well established. Children living in disharmonious homes show more emotional and behavioural problems than children living in harmonious homes. A study of 119 families (from the general population) with a child aged between nine and twelve years was carried out. Jenkins and Smith (1991) found parental conflict and disharmony as the strongest predictor of children's problems. Discrepancy in child-rearing practices was also a factor. These were obvious from the parents' and children's accounts of emotional and behavioural problems, such as indiscipline, insecurity, excessive competition, rivalry between children and social maladjustment.

The final complexity associated with the building of a negative character lies in the fact that the image of a subject is often an outcome of parochial, ethnocentric and orientalist viewpoints. In other words, it can be argued that historical or mythological villains might also have been treated in paradoxical manners. Their negative characteristics would have received much more attention by dominant intellectuals than their positive traits.

Another line of thought that may not directly apply on a macro level but has vast implications on individual behaviour comes from the Pygmalion effect. The Pygmalion effect refers to a phenomenon where people behave as expected of them. In a seminal study, Rosenthal and Jacobson (1968) demonstrated experimentally that a simple manipulation of teacher expectancy could improve pupil achievement. For example, in their experiment, the teachers were required to show higher expectations from certain students. This led the students to perform better.

In sum, drawing from the nurture vs nature theories, parochialism, ethnocentrism, orientalist perspectives and the Pygmalion effect, it can be argued that villains are either born, developed or simply made up. Therefore, Duryodhanization refers to the process of birth and subsequent development of a villainous character—whether in history or mythology. The larger questions that this book attempts to answer are:

a) Among various Duryodhanization processes, which ones explain the development of a particular individual as a villain?
b) Who are the beneficiaries of Duryodhanization?
c) What are the causes and processes of selection of a Duryodhana by the beneficiary?
d) What are the mechanisms that govern the process of Duryodhanization?
e) How does the beneficiary suppress resistance by a Duryodhana?
f) What are the advantages and disadvantages of such Duryodhanization?

Some critical disclaimers

Firstly, this book is a humble attempt to understand the process of Duryodhanization using certain historical or mythological characters. No differential treatment has been given to any character. In a sense it is unnecessary, at least for the purpose of this book. In fact, sometimes such common treatment is critical for philosophical inquiries. In the words of Munz (1956):

> In common usage the two words 'myth' and 'history' are used as if they denoted contradictories. A story is, so we are likely to be told, either true or false. If it is true, it is history; if it is false, it is a myth. Historians are inclined to call the version of an event which they consider untrue, a myth. They aim at replacing the products of human phantasy, mythology, by the products of historical research, history. There is no doubt some sense in such a simple distinction between history and myth. But it is apt to obscure a very important fact which has only too often been neglected. Myth and history, in a very special sense, are interdependent. They fertilize each other; and it is doubtful whether one could exist without the other.

Secondly, this book does not aim to establish any justification for wrongdoings by any mythological or historical villain. It is not even a process of falsification. It is simply an inquiry into certain processes that are theoretically and scientifically well-established explanations for the systematic image deterioration of certain macro-level phenomenon, (e.g. Indian caste system, nation, or a historical period) applied to mythological or historical villains. Additionally, the possibility of genetic and experiential development of villains is recognized.

Lastly, the book randomly selects some villainous characters from mythology or history. No scientific sample selection has been applied. This builds focus by narrowing the scope of the book. Nonetheless, three limiting mechanisms are applied in the random selection of characters. Drawing from history, characters are chosen from broadly defined historical periods: ancient history, the postclassical era and modern history. The second limitation is that the book only considers characters from Indian mythology and history. This is mostly convenient sampling. However, it is critical to avoid controversies. Readers are required to be mindful of the above limitations.

References

Boyacigiller, N.A., and Adler, N.J. (1991). The Parochial Dinosaur: Organizational Science in a Global Context. *Academy of Management Review* 16(2): 262–90.

Cirincione, J., Matthews, J.T., Perkovich, G., and Orton, A. (2004). WMD in Iraq: Evidence and Implications. *Biosecurity and Bioterrorism: Biodefense Strategy, Practice, and Science* 2(1): 51–55.

Curtius, E.R. (2013). *European Literature and the Latin Middle Ages*. Princeton University Press.

Dodds, K. (2005). Screening Geopolitics: James Bond and the Early Cold War Films (1962–67). *Geopolitics* 10(2): 266–89.

Gandhi, M.K. (1966). *Collected Works*, April–August 1921, Government of India. Ahmedabad: Navajivan Trust.

Gimpel, J. (1977). *The Medieval Machine: The Industrial Revolution of the Middle Ages*. New York: Penguin Books.

Grant, A.M., and Schwartz, B. (2011). Too Much of a Good Thing: The Challenge and Opportunity of the Inverted U. *Perspectives on Psychological Science* 6(1): 61–76.

Hofstede, G. (1981). Culture and Organizations. *International Studies of Management and Organizations* 10(4): 15–41.

Jinks, J.L., and Fulker, D.W. (1970). Comparison of the Biometrical Genetical, MAVA, and Classical Approaches to the Analysis of the Human Behavior. *Psychological Bulletin* 73(5): 311.

Jones, E.E., and Nisbett, R.E. (1971). *The Actor and the Observer: Divergent Perceptions of the Causes of Behavior*. Morristown, NJ: General Learning Press.

Kavoori, P.S. (2002). The Varna Trophic System: An Ecological Theory of Caste Formation. *Economic and Political Weekly* 1156–64.

Kull, S., Ramsay, C., and Lewis, E. (2003). Misperceptions, the Media, and the Iraq War. *Political Science Quarterly* 118(4): 569–98.

Lee, J. (2007). North Korea, South Korea, and 007 Die Another Day. *Critical Discourse Studies* 4(2): 207–35.

LeVine, Robert A., and Campbell, Donald T. (1972). *Ethnocentrism: Theories of Conflict, Ethnic Attitudes, and Group Behavior*. New York: Wiley.

Munz, P. (1956). History and Myth. *The Philosophical Quarterly* 6(22): 1–16.

Pierce, J.R., and Aguinis, H. (2013). The too-much-of-a-good-thing Effect in Management. *Journal of Management* 39(2): 313–38.

Rhee, S.H., and Waldman, I.D. (2002). Genetic and Environmental Influences on Antisocial Behavior: A Meta-Analysis of Twin and Adoption Studies. *Psychological Bulletin* 128(3): 490.

Robert, J. (2010). *Why Intelligence Fails: Lessons from the Iranian Revolution and the Iraq War*. Ithaca, NY: Cornell University Press.

Rosenthal, R., and Jacobson, L. (1968). *Pygmalion in the Classroom: Teacher Expectation and Pupils' Intellectual Development*. New York: Holt, Rinehart and Winston.

Said, E. (1979). *Orientalism*. New York: Vintage.

Shin, B., and Namkung, G. (2008). Films and Cultural Hegemony: American Hegemony 'Outside' and 'Inside' the '007' movie series. *Asian Perspective* 115–43.

Sumner, W.G. (1906). *Folkways: The Sociological Importance of Usages, Manners, Customs, Mores, and Morals*. New York: Ginn and Co.

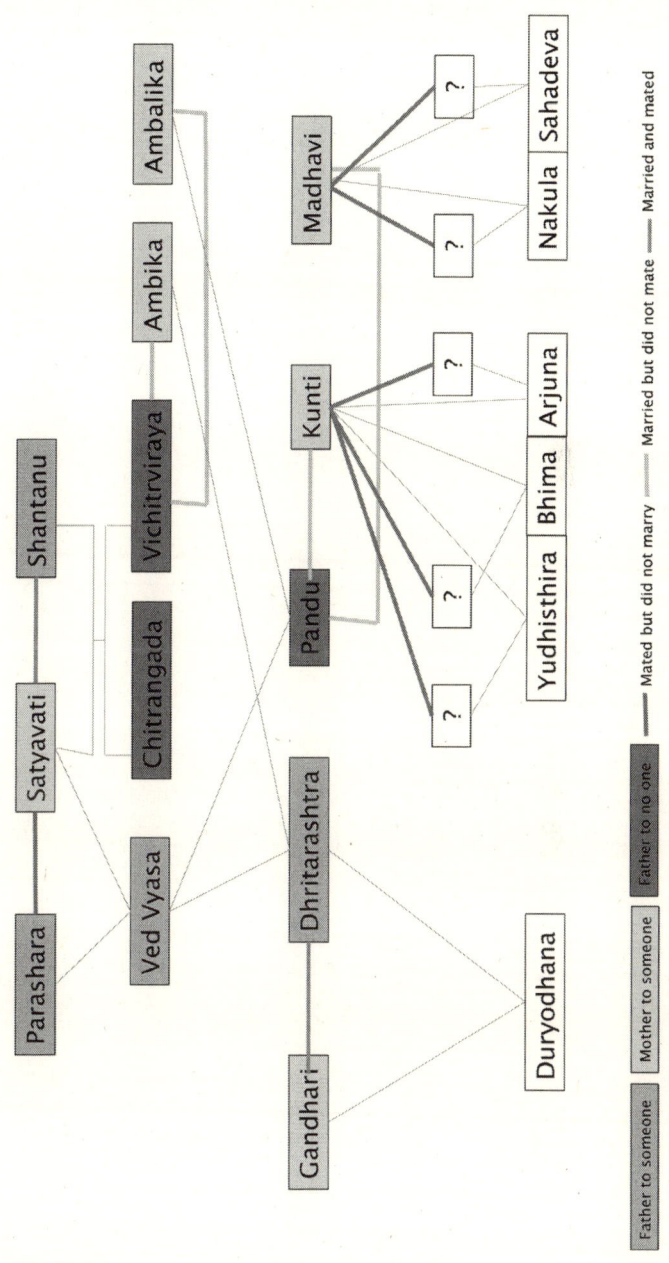

Figure 1

I

THE USUAL SUSPECTS

*Personality Traits Responsible for
Villainous Behaviour*

'Personality is something and personality does something.' Allport's (1937, p. 49)

In modern psychology and behavioural sciences, the study of personality traits or dispositions is a well-acknowledged method of studying human personality and behaviour. Traits can be defined as habitual patterns of behaviour, thought and emotion.[1] As per this definition, traits remain stable over time, differ amongst individuals and affect human behaviour in public and personal lives. Gordon Allport was amongst the first few recognized psychologists to advance the study of traits and dispositions. According to him, 'cardinal' traits are those that influence a person's behaviour and their ruling passions/obsessions. These traits can be positive or negative.

According to Bouchard and Loehlin, personality traits are major reflections of 'causal agency' embedded in humans by evolutionary processes.[2] Humans, like all other higher organisms, have been shaped by two major determinants of evolution. These are natural selection and sexual selection. They have been designed to transact actively with their

3

environments in order to survive and reproduce. According to this view, development of a particular personality trait in an individual is influenced, triggered and moderated by both proximal (e.g. genetics, family and peer group) and distal (e.g. sociopolitical environment and religious orientation) causes.

A significant amount of personality development research has shown that different dimensions and traits of personality are influenced by genotype and inheritance. Individual differences are inheritable. This means that genetic influences make a substantial contribution to individual differences in peoples' observable characteristics (or 'phenotypes'). In a meta-analysis of thirteen studies based on twins' samples, Loehlin (1976) found that significant variance in twins' behaviour was caused by genotypes. The studies were heterogeneous with respect to the type of personality measurements and background data for the subject groups. This significantly enhanced the validity of the study. This research identified several inheritable personality attributes such as inhibition, aggression, social extraversion, masculinity-femininity and maturity. The typical conclusion of such studies is that about 50 per cent of the observed variance in personality was due to genetic factors.[3]

Additionally, more recent theoretical and empirical work in personality research, behaviour genetics and evolutionary psychology has put considerable meat on the bare bones of this perceptive argument. Molecular genetics is poised to make its own contributions. This phenomenon is so universal that Turkheimer (2000)[4] enshrined it as the first law of behavioural genetics. Turkheimer went on to propose second and third laws as well. The second law states that being raised in the same family has a smaller effect on individual differences than genetic effects.

The third law states that a non-trivial portion of individual differences can be attributed to the unique nature of each individual. These go beyond genetic differences and being raised in the same family. These so-called laws indicate that the personality traits in an individual develop sequentially—first by genetics and subsequently by family and society.

Psychologists and behaviour scientists further explain that personality traits shape an individual's experience of feelings. These are described in terms such as 'elated', 'fearful', or 'sad' (Watson, 2000).[5] These experiences are popularly called trait affects. In this framework, affectivity exists along two separate unipolar dimensions (i.e. factors)—positive affect and negative affect. Higher positive affectivity is associated with experiencing a preponderance of positive feelings such as enthusiasm, alertness and joviality. And lower positive affectivity is related to feelings of lethargy and sluggishness. Higher levels of negative affectivity are associated with negative feelings such as guilt, fear, anxiety and nervousness. Meanwhile, lower negative affectivity is related to feelings such as serenity and calmness (Watson et al, 1988)[6]. Consistent with its definition of being enduring in nature, evidence indicates that a trait or dispositional affect is significantly inheritable. Genetic influences account for 40 per cent of the observed variance in positive effects and 55 per cent of variance in negative effects (Tellegen et al, 1988).[7]

Literature (e.g. Penny and Spector, 2005[8] and Skarlicki et al, 1999[9]) suggests that traits associated with negative affectivity leads to behaviour such as anger, social damage for pleasure, unwarranted and extravagant retaliation, revengefulness, lower social commitment and incivility. In colloquial terms, the combination of the above behavioural characteristics can be called villain-some.

Well-established traits that represent negative affectivity in individuals include Machiavellianism, neuroticism, narcissism, psychopathy and everyday sadism. These traits lead to increased villainous behaviour that mostly has a negative impact on the surrounding environment. In the following sections, I will discuss these negative human dispositions.

1

Machiavellianism

Niccolò Machiavelli (1469–1527) was a Florentine diplomat who visited the courts of Europe, and observed first-hand the rise and fall of leaders. His own fall came with the overthrow of the regime that he served. He wrote *The Prince* (Machiavelli, 1513/1966) to ingratiate himself with the contemporary ruler. *The Prince* is a book of advice on how to acquire and stay in power. It is based entirely on expediency and is devoid of the traditional virtues of trust, honour and decency. A line from the book reads, 'Men are so simple and so much inclined to obey immediate needs that a deceiver will never lack victims for his deceptions' (p. 63). The term Machiavellianism refers to the infamous Niccolò Machiavelli. This notorious book espoused his view that strong rulers should be harsh with their subjects and enemies. And that glory and survival justified any means, even ones considered to be immoral and brutal.

Machiavelli failed to gain favour with the new prince. His name, however, has come to represent a strategy of social conduct, which others regard as means towards personal ends. By the late sixteenth century, Machiavellianism was a popular word to describe the art of being deceptive to get ahead. But it wasn't a psychological term until the 1970s when two social psychologists, Richard Christie and Florence L. Geis developed what they called the 'Machiavellianism scale'. A personality test that is still used as the main assessment tool for Machiavellianism, this scale is now called 'the Mach-IV test'. Christie and Geis (1968, 1970, and 1970) were the first psychologists to study Machiavellianism as an important axis of human behavioural variation. They developed a series of Mach tests that measured a participant's agreement with statements such as 'never tell anyone the real reason you did something unless it is useful to do so.' High and low scorers on the test, often referred to as high-Machs and low-Machs, differ in many other aspects of their behaviour like vocational choices and success in team games.

More recently, Machiavellianism has become a term of interest in evolutionary biology. Several authors have speculated that for higher primates, social interactions are by far the most challenging aspect of the environment. And that they were a major factor in the evolution of human intelligence as well (e.g. Byrne and Whiten, 1988; De Waal, 1982, 1986). The focus on social interactions contrasts with previous theories of intelligence and a long tradition in experimental psychology that studies intelligence in a non-social context. Evolutionary literature is full of interesting hypotheses on the adaptive value of manipulative behaviours. But it is short on experimental tests with humans and other species. On the other hand, psychological literature is full of empirical results on humans. However, it does not provide a conceptual framework that integrates the results and guides future research.

In psychology, Machiavellianism refers to a personality trait where a person is so focused on his/her own interests that they will manipulate others to achieve their personal goals. Machiavellianism is one of the traits in what is called the 'dark triad'. The other two are narcissism and psychopathy. These will be discussed in the following chapters. Common tendencies associated with Machiavellianism include being focused only on your own ambitions, prioritizing money and power over relationships, coming across as charming and confident, exploiting others to get what you want, lying and deceiving whenever required, using flattery to achieve your ends, lacking principles and values, coming across as aloof, being cynical of goodness and morality, being capable of causing others harm to achieve your own means, showing low levels of empathy, often avoiding commitment and emotional attachments, rarely revealing your true intentions, being prone to casual sexual encounters, showing a lack of warmth in social interactions, not always being aware of the consequences of your actions and finding it difficult to identify your own emotions.

Machiavellianism in social interactional psychology is defined as 'a strategy of social conduct that involves manipulating others for personal gain' (Christie and Geis, 1970, 285; Wilson et al, 1996).[1] 'Machiavellianism is a tendency towards manipulation, often accompanied by (a) a lack of empathy, (b) lower levels of affect, (c) a focus on pursuing one's own goals, and (d) an aberrant view of morality (i.e. one that offers a greater acceptance of behaviours that would normally be described as immoral or unethical, such as lying, manipulating and exploiting others' (Christie and Geis, 1970; Dahling et al, 2009; Kessler et al, 2010; Paulhus and Williams, 2002; Rauthmann and Will, 2011; Spain et al, 2014; Wu and LeBreton, 2011).[2] The construct of Machiavellianism is associated with diminished or absent affect in interpersonal relationships, amorality, psychological health and little commitment to an ideology.[3] Machiavellianism is also defined as 'social conduct that involves manipulating others for personal gain, often against the other's self-interest.'[4]

Machiavellianism involves a particular worldview and an application of certain behavioural methods and tactics. Machiavellian people characteristically attribute negative intentions to others and do not expect cooperation from them. They start out with the assumption that others will exploit them if they themselves fail to do so. They are capable of distracting themselves from the emotional effects of certain situations. They remain 'cool-blooded' even in highly charged emotional situations, and do not get affected by the excitement around them. This emotional coldness, again, contributes to the successful manipulation of others.[5]

2

NARCISSISM

Narcissism in its modern usage began as a clinical construct. When most individuals think of narcissism today, they probably see it as related to clinical theory. One of the earliest known clinical references to narcissism came from British sexologist, Havelock Ellis (1880). He used the term to describe the paraphilia of kissing or being sexually attracted to oneself. Narcissism grew into a more complex and far-reaching psychological variable with Freud's (1914/1957) *On Narcissism: An Introduction*. Freud spoke of narcissism in several ways. Most relevant to the current social psychological research, he described narcissism as a type of attachment to the self rather than to the other. He discussed narcissism in terms of regulating libido in such a way that all interpersonal relationships strengthen the positivity of the self, even at the expense of feelings of warmth and care for others. Most modern social psychologists would, for example, stray from Freud's use of conceptually vague terms such as 'libido'. However, Freud's contribution to modern social psychological theories regarding narcissism should not be overlooked. His focus on the narcissistic drive to regulate the self, using interpersonal tactics is one that continues to manifest itself in the modern social psychological literature.

Narcissism has been studied as an individual differences variable for almost as long as it has been considered a clinical condition. This is often forgotten in its intellectual history. Freud, for example, included narcissism as a basic personality feature in 'libidinal types'. Those of the narcissistic type were said to be confident, independent, energetic and aggressive. Wilhelm Reich (1949) also described a phallic-narcissistic character that was similar to Freud's. Finally, Henry Murray (1938) developed what, to our knowledge, was the first personality measure of narcissism. He also published the first correlations of narcissism with different outcome measures. Importantly, and in contrast to the clinical history of narcissism as a personality variable, narcissism was generally considered to be a normal trait rather than a pathological condition.

According to more modern psychologists, it is useful to think of narcissism as having three basic ingredients. These include a positive self, a relative lack of interest in warm and caring interpersonal relationships and a reliance upon self-regulatory strategies. Narcissism is one of the three dark triadic personality traits, as mentioned in the previous chapter. Except in the sense of primary narcissism or healthy self-love, narcissism is usually considered a problem in a person or a group's relationship with oneself and others.

Individuals with higher levels of narcissism are likely to (a) harbour feelings of superiority driven by an inflated sense of self, (b) have a dysfunctional need for excessive attention and admiration, (c) have a propensity to engage in exploitative acts and (d) lack empathy, tending toward callousness.[1]

Pincus et al (2009) referred to 'narcissistic grandiosity' as 'interpersonally exploitive acts, a lack of empathy, intense envy, aggression and exhibitionism'. He also added that 'narcissistic vulnerability', 'the conscious experience of helplessness, emptiness, low self-esteem and shame', represented another important aspect of narcissism.[2]

Narcissism can be defined as a 'relatively stable individual difference consisting of grandiosity, self-love and inflated self-views' (Campbell et al, 2011, 269).[3] In the eyes of narcissists, there is much about themselves that is enviable. Narcissists view themselves more positively than they view others, in terms of intelligence, competence and attractiveness. This tendency carries over to specific task performance related situations. Here, narcissists tend to self-enhance, and are more likely than others to derogate sources of negative performance feedback. These attributional biases are rooted in narcissists' strong motives to maintain a positive self-image and uphold the positive effect they experience from downward comparisons with others.

Contemporary conceptualizations of narcissism include both narcissistic grandiosity and narcissistic vulnerability.[4] Narcissistic vulnerability tendencies may be classified as a personality type characterized by a high and unstable self-esteem. Although the definition of narcissism overlaps with self-esteem, it has two distinctive characteristics that are not formally associated with the concept of self-esteem. These are competitiveness and the need for admiration. Thus, it involves maintaining high self-esteem by constant comparison with others. Narcissists are only satisfied when they outperform others or are given lavish praise by their admirers.

A great deal of speculation has gone into understanding the childhood roots of narcissism. There are three basic schools of thought (Horton et al, 2006). The first is that narcissists were psychologically wounded during childhood. They did not receive the attention that they needed (Kernberg, 1974, 1975; Kohut, 1977) and were controlled by their parents. A second position is that narcissists were overly attended to in childhood, in a fashion that led to psychological enmeshment. In essence, the child was used to act out the parents' own narcissistic needs (Kohut, 1977). The third is that narcissists were somehow spoiled in childhood, receiving too much positive regard and treated with inordinate leniency (Millon and Davis, 1996). The best empirical data available (Horton et al, 2006) is most consistent with the 'spoiled' portrayal of the narcissists' childhoods. In particular, parental leniency is seen as a significant predictor of narcissism. The Horton data was conceptually replicated in a similar study (Otway and Vignoles, 2006). Adults were asked about the nature of parenting they received in childhood. Narcissism was positively related to recollections of parental over-evaluation.

Narcissism is thus defined as a person's ability to maintain a positive view of the self through self-enhancement experiences. For example, they can downplay the skills that they lack, or they can criticize others to seem better by comparison, and vice versa. This particular aspect will throw some light on to our current discourse when we analyse four characters from the Mahabharata.

3

PSYCHOPATHY

Although the literal meaning of psychopathic is psychologically damaged, the term has long since been transmogrified to mean socially damaging. It implies a specific category of people inherently committed to antisocial behaviour as a consequence of personal abnormalities or deficiencies.

The origins of recent notions of psychopathic personality are commonly traced to Prichard's (1837) concept of moral insanity (Maughs, 1941). Prichard merely elaborated the proposals of the eighteenth-century physicians. His implication of the term 'moral' went beyond just 'ethical' (Walker and McCabe, 1973; Millon, 1981). His illustrative cases included only a few, for whom antisocial conduct was the chief reason for inferring moral insanity. Nevertheless, he tried to explain socially objectionable behaviour. He talked of it as an inability to conduct oneself 'with decency and propriety in the business of life', referring to moral 'perversion'. Moral insanity was thus a hypothetical cause of social deviance. And much of the subsequent debate in the nineteenth century centred on how a diseased 'moral faculty' could explain criminal behaviour.

Walker and McCabe (1973) detect three differing uses of the term psychopathy. Initially, it had the etymologically precise meaning of 'psychologically damaged', hence comprising all forms of psychopathology. However, in 1891 Koch described psychological abnormalities that did not amount to strict insanity as 'constitutional psychopathic inferiority'. This was an explicit rejection of the notion of moral insanity as well as an attempt to specify a biological basis for non-psychotic disorders. The third use of the term was to mean 'unethical'. This is attributed to Meyer's influence in the USA and Henderson's in Britain. However, this narrow application did not become widespread for several decades.

Walker and McCabe (1973) suggest that the original intention was for psychopathic disorder to be a generic label for non-psychotic psychiatric disorders, but the antisocial connotations had become too entrenched. In practice, those who fall in the category of psychopathic disorder tend to have committed socially abhorrent crimes. They are indiscriminately labelled as psychopaths.

A four-dimensional model offered by Williams et al (2007) summarizes 'psychopathy along four key dimensions: interpersonal manipulation, callous affect, erratic lifestyle and criminal tendencies (e.g. antisocial or counterproductive behaviour)'.[1] It is a personality trait characterized by enduring antisocial behaviour, diminished empathy and remorse, and disinhibited, bold behaviour.[2]

Psychologists define psychopathy as a particular constellation of antisocial behaviour and emotions, including shallow affect, low remorse, low fear, low empathy, egocentrism, exploitative instinct, manipulativeness, impulsivity, aggression and criminality (Cleckley, 1964; Hare, 1993). Much like the psychological construct of narcissism, psychopathy has been extensively studied by both clinical and personality psychologists. Generally, researchers believe there are two factors of psychopathy. The first factor is called primary or instrumental psychopathy. This results in shallow affect, low empathy and interpersonal coldness. Individuals with profound levels of these traits are sometimes referred to as 'emotionally stable' psychopaths. The second factor is secondary or hostile/reactive psychopathy. This is composed of socially manipulative and deviant facets of psychopathy. It has been referred to as aggressive, impulsive and neurotic psychopathy.[3]

Psychopathy is described as a syndrome of extreme interpersonal, affective and behavioural traits. Some researchers argue that the concept of psychopathy should not include criminal behaviour. It could be seen as a potential consequence rather than as a part of the personality syndrome of psychopathy.[4] The primary tendencies include impulsive thrill-seeking, cold affect, manipulation and antisocial behaviours, often falling into a primary (affective shallowness, lack of empathy and remorse, superficial charm, and manipulation) and secondary component (social deviance, low socialization, impulsivity, irresponsibility, aggression, sensation seeking, delinquency).[5]

In terms of lifestyles, psychopaths lack realistic life goals, have parasitic orientations, are altogether irresponsible and impulsive, and seek stimulation. In conduct, psychopaths have poor behavioural control, evince early behaviour problems, engage in juvenile delinquency, are criminally versatile, and have records of noncompliance/revocation of conditional release. When charged with their crimes, they present themselves as guiltless and are prone to externalize blame.[6]

It appears that psychopathy has remained, more or less, a pejorative label. However, the most recent debate among scholars entails the use of more behavioural criteria than personality traits to effectively diagnose psychiatric illnesses. Notwithstanding its evolution, two features of this mental disorder have remained relatively constant. First, the presence of psychosis is an essential criterion for the existence of psychopathy. Second, psychopathic individuals are generally considered untreatable. Some researchers have debated the fate of psychopaths in asylums or prisons. Most agree that their dispositions are largely unchangeable. Given the foregoing historical analysis, we are yet to see the implications of present-day correctional and psychological practice for psychopaths.

4

NEUROTICISM

Neuroticism, as an aspect of human personality in various forms, has been a subject of study for thousands of years. In ancient Greece, personality types were categorized into four basic temperaments: choleric, melancholic, phlegmatic and sanguine. The melancholic personality had many traits associated with neuroticism. Greek doctor Hippocrates (460–370 BC) suggested a biological basis for personality. He claimed that melancholy was caused by excessive amounts of black bile in the body. More recently, neuroticism has formed the basis of numerous personality models.

German-born psychologist Hans Eysenck (1916–97) also believed that personality traits were attributable to biological factors. He developed a model that quantified personality according to two dimensions: extraversion and neuroticism. In modern psychometric studies of personality and psychopathology, neuroticism tends to be identified as a first general factor (i.e. the biggest variable in explaining individual differences). For example, a large percentage of variability in the types of mental illness characterized as 'internalizing', such as depression, anxiety, obsessive-compulsive neurosis, phobia, and hysteria, can be explained by a general dimension of neuroticism. Thus, neuroticism almost always appears in modern trait models of personality, though sometimes with slightly different theoretical formulations or names (such as trait anxiety, repression-sensitization, ego-resiliency, and negative emotionality). Eysenck popularized the term neuroticism in the 1950s by including it as a key scale in his popular personality inventory.

Neuroticism figures prominently in the widely accepted big five model of personality disposition (a model that considers five factors to produce its assessment: openness to experience, conscientiousness, extraversion, agreeableness, and neuroticism). It is measured on a continuum, ranging from emotional stability (low neuroticism) to emotional instability (high neuroticism). A neurotic personality is characterized by persistent, often disproportionate, worrying and anxiety. A person may strive to be a perfectionist during their everyday activities, experiencing stress as a result of events beyond their control. Neuroticism can cause an individual to dwell on the negative aspects of a situation rather than the positive ones. They feel envious towards other people when they feel they are in a position of advantage as compared to them. They may be prone to frustration, irritation and anger as they struggle to cope with the stresses of life.

Some define neuroticism as a tendency to be aroused quickly when stimulated and to gain slow relaxation from arousal. Others define it as emotional instability, negativity or maladjustment as compared to emotional stability, positivity or good adjustment. Still others define it as lack of self-control, poor ability to manage psychological stress and a tendency to complain.[1]

Neuroticism signifies the tendency to experience negative emotions such as guilt, nervousness, depression and fear. It involves behaviour such as lack of self-acceptance, perfectionism, and not being open to criticism (Costa and McCrae, 1995).[2] Individuals who score low in neuroticism tend to be more emotionally stable and less reactive to stress. They tend to be calm, even-tempered and less likely to feel tense or rattled. Although they are low in negative emotion, they are not necessarily high in positive emotion.

Scoring high in positive emotion is generally an element of the independent trait of extraversion. Neurotic extraverts, for example, would experience high levels of both positive and negative emotional states. An 'emotional roller coaster' of sorts.[3][4]

Alec Roy[5] demonstrated that neuroticism is an important personality dimension associated with depressive and anxiety disorders. Both genetic and social factors are thought to contribute to neuroticism. His study aims to examine whether early childhood adversity may be a determinant of neuroticism. He made 532 abstinent substance-dependent patients complete the childhood trauma questionnaire (CTQ) and the Eysenck personality questionnaire (EPQ). The result of the survey showed a significant relationship between total childhood trauma scores on the CTQ and neuroticism scores on the EPQ. There was also a significant correlation between neuroticism and CTQ sub-scores for emotional abuse, physical abuse, sexual abuse, emotional neglect and physical neglect. To conclude his study, he claimed that childhood trauma may be a determinant of neuroticism. This could be one way in which childhood trauma plays a role in the development of psychiatric disorders.

Accruing research data show that individual differences in neuroticism are substantially inheritable (which means they can be passed on from parent to child). Inheritability estimates based on twin studies generally fall in the 40–60 per cent range. The remaining individual differences in neuroticism are primarily attributed to unique (non-familial) environmental differences. The shared familial environment appears to exert virtually no reliable influence on individual differences in neuroticism. Researchers speculate that an overreactive limbic system in the brain is associated with high levels of neuroticism. An overreactive limbic system signifies excessive reactions to usual and day-to-day stimuli, and manifests in the individual's emotions and motivations. However, specific neurochemical mechanisms or locations within the brain and nervous system have not yet been identified.

5

EVERYDAY SADISTS

Everyday sadists are distinguished not by their impulsiveness or manipulativeness (which are in the normal range), but by their enjoyment of cruelty. Sadism is essentially defined as the derivation of pleasure from the physical or emotional suffering of another, or from the control and domination of others.[1] Sadists have also been described as aggressive or malignant narcissists, as their pleasure is derived at the expense of others with no apparent concern for their well-being.[2]

Unlike psychopaths, they rarely use physical force in the commission of crimes. Their aggressiveness is embedded in an interpersonal context and expressed in social settings, such as the family or the workplace. This narcissistic need for an audience manifests itself in other circumstances. Sadists strive to humiliate people in front of witnesses. This makes the sadist feel omnipotent. Power is important to them. And they are likely to treat people under their control or entrusted to their care harshly, be it a subordinate, child, student, prisoner, patient or spouse. They are all liable to suffer the consequences of the sadist's 'control freak attitude' and exacting 'disciplinary' measures. Sadists like to inflict pain because they find suffering, both corporeal and psychological, amusing. The sights and sounds of a creature writhing in agony are pleasurable to them. Sadists go to great lengths to hurt others. They lie, deceive, commit crimes and even make personal sacrifices merely to enjoy the cathartic moment of witnessing someone else's misery. Masters of abuse by proxy, they terrorize even their dear ones into doing their bidding. They create an atmosphere of dread and consternation by promulgating complex 'rules of the house' that restrict the autonomy of their dependants (spouses, children, employees, patients, clients, etc.) They have the final word and their decisions must be obeyed, no matter how senseless.

Psychologists talk about the dark triad in personality, representing a perfect-storm combination of narcissism, psychopathy, and Machiavellianism. People high in the dark triad traits callously use people to their own advantage, seeing them as tools to be exploited in order to get what they want. To be sure, enjoying the suffering of others—the hallmark of sadism—can be a part of the picture in the dark triad constellation. However, personality psychologists are beginning to believe that a predilection for cruelty stands on its own in understanding why one person would want to harm another. Along with behaviour that results in humiliation, maiming or death, there's a kind of everyday sadism that shows up in a more benign form.

University of British Columbia psychologist Erin Buckels and collaborators (2013)[3] decided to investigate the idea that everyday sadists are willing to inflict real, not just vicarious, harm. They reasoned that people with high levels of this less overt form of sadism might become more aggressive when provoked than other individuals. Further, they believed that sadism could provide unique predictions of antisocial behaviour, above and beyond those of the dark triad qualities. To investigate everyday sadism, they needed to come up with a laboratory task that would mimic the kind of casual, harm-producing behaviour people might perform in their daily lives. But translating everyday sadism into a lab setting is, understandably, a challenge. You have to invent a task that will not actually hurt people but which will seem realistic. Buckels and her team zeroed in on killing bugs. They argued that the act of killing a bug would satisfy a sadistic desire to cause a living creature harm through direct physical contact.

To test their theory, they offered participants a choice of tasks. Killing bugs was one of the alternatives among a set of unpleasant but non-sadistic options. They settled on three choices (including killing bugs) a participant could pick as possible 'jobs'—assisting someone else in killing bugs, cleaning dirty toilets or putting their hand in a bucket of ice water. (In case you're worried, bugs weren't actually killed. But it looked like the bugs were supposedly ground in a machine that loudly crunched them to bits.)

To identify the everyday sadists in the sample, Buckels and her team used the short sadistic impulse scale (SSIS) developed by University of College Cork psychologist Aisling O'Meara and her team (2011).[4] They also administered dark triad questionnaires to tease out the separate contributions of sadism from the other two qualities. As expected, participants who scored high on sadism were the most likely to choose the bug-killing task. After completing the task, they also reported enjoying it the most. And if they had opted for a different task, they regretted not choosing bug killing in the first place.

The second laboratory task involved a button-pushing competition. The highly sadistic participants were compared with their less cruel counterparts in their willingness to attack an opponent who they believed would not attack them back. Over the course of the experiment, participants had the opportunity to blast white noise into their opponent's headphones for every trial that they won. The situation was rigged as there was no actual opponent. However, the participants were led to believe that their opponent would not attack them back after receiving the ear-disrupting blast.

The question then, was whether those who were highly sadistic would continue to inflict the aversive stimulus upon a non-attacking opponent. As it turned out, the everyday sadists were not only quicker to harm their opponents but also worked harder for the opportunity to blast them some more. Dark triad qualities, as in the bug-killing experiment, didn't predict the outcome of noise-blasting tendencies. However, sadism did. We have fairly solid evidence now that people who score high on a questionnaire measure of sadism may also behave in casual, everyday ways that might be similar to these lab tasks. The questionnaire measure appears to have a reasonably good validity in predicting who would kill for the sake of killing (bugs, of course, not people) and who would inflict harm on an opponent who is offering an olive branch.

Although sadistic personalities seem to be an increasing percentage of the aggressive personality types in prison settings, they do not appear to be very common in the general population. Nonetheless, they cause an inordinate amount of distress for those who happen to become entangled in some kind of relationship with them. Traditional theories on personality development have always presumed that sadistic individuals became the way they are because of deep-seated feelings of inferiority, or as a reaction to being severely abused or demeaned as children. But there is no evidence to suggest that all such personalities have these characteristics in their background, although many will lie about it to engender the sympathy of others. It seems that the majority of these individuals simply consider themselves superior to those whom they perceive as weak.

Paulhus notes that everyday sadists may be drawn to jobs such as police officers or the military, where they can harm others in a legitimate guise.[5] This is not to suggest that all law-enforcement personnel are sadistic, simply that their ranks may have a higher than average number of everyday sadists.

In summary, the independent or collective presence of Machiavellianism, narcissism, neuroticism, psychopathy and everyday sadism in a person can significantly influence that individual's behaviour negatively. Collectively, these personality traits can be a perfect recipe for disaster. These personality traits are largely hereditarily transmittable. Therefore, the presence of these traits in an individual can generally be traced back to the genes.

II

THE KURUS

Personality Assessments of Common Lineage

1

THE DYDE

Satyavati and Shantanu

Satyavati: An Insecure Mother

Not much has been mentioned about Satyavati in the Mahabharata. Despite her low-caste origins, she changed the fate of the royal hierarchy of Hastinapur. A little bit has been written about her in Harivamsa, and more so in the Devi Bhagavata Purana.[1] All the texts mention Satyavati's fisherman father. He was the reason behind Bhishma's pledge and the eventual downfall of Hastinapur. Some scholars consider Satyavati, and not her father, responsible for both of these. While her presence of mind, far-sightedness and mastery of realpolitik are praised, her unscrupulous means of achieving her goals and her blind ambition are criticized.

Satyavati was the biological daughter of Uparichara Vasu, a Gandharva king. He refused to take her with him as she was born out of a fish (a cursed nymph called Aadrika) according to mythology. Eventually, she was adopted by the chief of the fishermen clan, Dasharaja. She used to row the boat on the Yamuna to cross the river where she met Maharishi Parashara. By satisfying his sexual desire, she turned from Matsyagandha to Yojanagandha.[2] After marrying King Shantanu of Hastinapur, she became the queen of Hastinapur.

There are certain noteworthy instances in the Mahabharata that highlight Satyavati's behaviour and enable us to ascertain the kind of personality traits she exhibited. The first incident was her encounter with the sage Parashara. Pradip Bhattacharya (2004) praises Satyavati's handling of this encounter. He notes that, although young, she tackles the persistent sage with great maturity and presence of mind. Bhattacharya remarks, 'With a maturity and frankness that astonishes us even in the twenty-first century, she points out that coitus ought to be mutually enjoyable.' (Bhattacharya, 2004) She is not deluded by the belief that the sage will marry her and in exchange for her virginity, tries to raise her future status in society.

The second incident when she showed her 'characteristic far-sightedness' and ensured the future of her children with Shantanu was by indirectly deposing off the crown prince Bhishma.[3] Some scholars such as Indrajeet Bandopadhyaya (2013) opine that Satyavati did not have 'spiritual merit' as she manipulated Shantanu by hiding her previous encounter with sage Parashara. And her adopted father Dasharaja stepped in to fix the prerequisites of her marriage. This led to the dispossession of Bhishma's right as the heir apparent to the throne, while Satyavati played the coy lady who would not go against her father to protest the injustice done to Bhishma.[4] Kisari Mohan Ganguli, in his English translation of the Mahabharata of Krishna Dwaipayana, describes this as: 'The fisherman said, "O king, what I ask of thee is this: the son born of this maiden shall be installed by thee on thy throne and none else shall thou make thy successor."'[5]

For Satyavati, the end justified the means. Her life's ambition became the assurance of succession of Shantanu's lineage and inheritance of his fortune by her sons. But ironically, Bhishma, whose right to the throne was snatched away because of her, outlived her children in life and in fame. Her actions indirectly created a generation encompassed by greed, which ultimately led to its annihilation. Dhanalakshmi Ayyer concludes that 'Satyavati's story teaches the new generation women that determination and commitment are different from avarice and calculation. One should know where greed takes over from ambition.' (Ayyer, 2006)[6]

The third instance that depicted her personality was how even after her marriage to Shantanu, she never revealed the truth about her illegitimate son Vyasa. His birth was the consequence of her encounter with Parashara. She was afraid that telling the truth might anger Shantanu and lead him to further suspect that their sons, Chitrangada and Vichitravirya, were also not his. Satyavati's insecurity towards her sons' rights as heirs was the reason behind the manipulation and machinations she used against Shantanu. She was afraid of losing the importance and acceptance that he gave her, as she had been deprived of it in her early years. The difficulties of growing up as a girl in the Vedic era cannot be ignored. On the threshold of adolescence, Satyavati dealt with foster parents, difficult sages, sexual awakening and loneliness. Yearning to be loved and treasured, and not willing to be treated as a lackey despite her royal descent, Satyavati set out to create her own destiny.

The fourth instance was when, to ensure that Bhishma does not control the entire administration in the absence of her sons, she did not send Vichitravirya and Chitrangada to a gurukul to pursue formal education as was necessary in those days for Kshatriya princes.[7] That was the scale of her insecurity. She also refused to let Bhishma be her sons' teacher. This was because she was afraid that he might take revenge by harming them and teaching them what they should not learn as princes: selflessness, spirituality and humility. Here again, Satyavati's insecurity and envy towards Bhishma is evident.

After analyzing the first and second behavioural instances, it seems that Satyavati exhibited Machiavellian personality traits. The second and third instances show that Satyavati was also narcissistic in character. The third, fourth and the fifth instances further substantiate that she seemed to be neurotic in her behaviour.

Ayyer describes Satyavati as 'the embodiment of the driving force of womanhood, with motherly ambition blinding her vision at every turn' and adds that 'in a way, Satyavati exemplifies what Rudyard Kipling succinctly put: "The female of the species must be deadlier than the male."' (Ayyer, 2006)[8]

Shantanu: A Guilt-ridden Father

Shantanu had his own merits and demerits. His acceptance of various controversial conditions imposed on him for marrying Ganga and then Satyavati is indicative of his disposition. Some of these tendencies are highlighted below.

The first instance that outlines Shantanu's negative traits was when he fell in love with Ganga. He asked her to become his wife and the queen of Hastinapur, to which she gladly agreed. Ganguli translates the Sanskrit text in Mahabharata as:

Of faultless features, the damsel sending a thrill of pleasure into the heart by every word she uttered, said, 'O king, I shall become thy wife and obey thy commands. But, O monarch, thou must not interfere with me in anything I do, be it agreeable or disagreeable. Nor shall thou ever address me unkindly. As long as thou shalt behave kindly I promise to live with thee. But I shall certainly leave thee the moment thou interferest with me or speakest to me an unkind word.

The king answered, 'Be it so.' And thereupon the damsel obtaining that excellent monarch, foremost in the Bharata race, as her husband became highly pleased. And king Shantanu also, obtaining her for his wife, enjoyed to the full the pleasure of her company. And adhering to his promise, he refrained from asking her anything. And the lord of earth, Shantanu, became exceedingly gratified with her conduct, beauty, magnanimity, and attention to his comforts. . . And she gratified the king by her attractiveness and affection, by her wiles and love, by her music and dance, and became herself gratified. And the monarch was so enraptured with his beautiful wife that months, seasons, and years rolled on without his being conscious of them.[9]

These lines depict Shantanu's willingness to marry Ganga and his lust to have her by all means, even if it meant staking his whole kingdom. This shows how flawed he was, as a king and as a virtuous human being.

The second instance which throws light on his personality is when he lets Ganga drown their sons in the river as soon as they are born, without questioning her actions. Even though his expressions clearly showed how unhappy and frustrated he felt, he did not utter a single word. He finally lost his patience when Ganga tried to drown their eighth son, Devvrata (later known as Bhishma due to his terrible vow of celibacy). He stopped her from doing so and questioned her as to why she had done this to all their sons.

In his work, Ganguli describes it as:

And the king, while thus enjoying himself with his wife, had eight children born unto him who in beauty were like the very celestials themselves. But, O Bharata, those children, one after another, as soon as they were born, were thrown into the river by Ganga who said, 'This is for thy good.' And the children sank to rise no more. The king, however, could not be pleased with such conduct. But he spoke not a word about it lest his wife should leave him. But when the eighth child was born, and when his wife as before was about to throw it smilingly into the river, the king with a sorrowful countenance and desirous of saving it from destruction, addressed her and said, 'Kill it not! Who art thou and whose? Why dost thou kill thy own children? Murderess of thy sons, the load of thy sins is great!'[10]

The third instance that shows his character traits is when he falls in love with Satyavati after Ganga leaves him. When he sees Satyavati for the first time, he wants to marry her. She asks him to seek her father's permission first. Satyavati's adoptive father puts forward a condition to Shantanu. He has to fulfill it in order to marry his daughter. In the guise of security for Satyavati and her future sons, it actually calls for injustice to Bhishma. Ganguli translates these lines in the Mahabharata as: 'The fisherman said, "O king, what I ask of thee is this: the son born of this maiden shall be installed by thee on thy throne and none else shall thou make thy successor."'[11] He did not agree to this condition right away but he was so disheartened by it that he lost his zest for life and became a recluse. Seeing his father's condition Bhishma tries to find out the reason behind his misery. As soon as he finds out, he reaches Satyavati's home to seek her hand from her father on Shantanu's behalf. When her father lays down the same condition as he laid down before Shantanu, Bhishma agrees to it. He further takes a vow of lifelong celibacy so that his heirs never claim a right over the throne of Hastinapur. Even though Shantanu is shocked to hear about Bhishma's terrible vow and his relinquishment of the throne, he is happy from within to have Satyavati as his wife. He does not ask Bhishma to take back his vow but gives him a boon that he can only die at will. This shows how his carnal desires prevailed over his fatherly duties (by allowing the injustice meted out to Bhishma). Ganguli translates Vaisampayana's words as:

> And Shantanu also, hearing of the extraordinary achievements of his son, became highly gratified and bestowed upon the high-souled prince the boon of death at will, saying, 'Death shall never come to thee as long as thou desirest to live. Truly death shall approach thee, O sinless one, having first obtained thy command.[12]

His character is also reflected in his helplessness to do anything that might make Satyavati unhappy. He fulfills every wish of hers, be it her wish to not send her sons to gurukul for formal education or not allowing Bhishma to become their sons' teacher.

The above instances highlight signs of the presence of various negative personality traits such as narcissism and neuroticism.

Satyavati and Shantanu: A Dyad Analysis

Research on the impact of couple or inter-parental conflict on children has a long established history.[13] For as long back as the 1930s, it has been recognized that discord between parents has a potentially debilitating effect on children's psychological development.[14] Conflict between parents is understood to affect the dynamic of the entire family.[15] Disagreement in marriages will inevitably arise, but it is the way the parents choose to respond to discord that has a positive or negative impact on the child.[16] Research has characterized negative marital conflict as comprised five factors: intensity, frequency, consistency, content and resolution. In this context negative marital conflict is consistent over time, characterized by child-centred content, high in intensity, frequently occurring and lacking in a visible resolution to the child. Negative conflict between parents is detrimental to their children's social, emotional and cognitive developments. It can damage their relationship with their parents.[17]

Periodic conflict between couples is natural and something most children will be exposed to at some point in their lives without necessarily experiencing adverse effects. However, research indicates frequent, intense and poorly resolved couple conflict is very harmful for children.

Recent research has highlighted how children's exposure to discordant, but non-violent conflict between parents also exerts negative effects on their development (Cummings and Davies, 2010, Rhoades, 2008).[18] Research supports the proposal that practitioners and policymakers should move away from considering conflict between parents as a simple present or absent dichotomy (i.e. violent or not). It acknowledges that conflicted behaviour between parents exists across a continuum of expressed severity, ranging from hostile silence to physical violence.

Emery (1982) reviewed the connections between marital turmoil and behavioural problems in children.[19] How one defined conflict, whether in intact or broken families, was a matter of controversy. Three theoretically relevant aspects of conflict are the form of the conflict (e.g. hitting, arguing and avoidance), the content of the conflict (e.g. sex, child rearing, money, etc.) and its duration. Both, the amount and type of inter-parental conflict to which the child is exposed to, seem to be important determinants of the effect on the child. Conflict that is openly hostile exposes the child to more, presumably problematic, parental interactions. As does conflict that lasts for a long period of time. Emery concluded, in part, that marital turmoil is more strongly related to maladaptive behaviour in boys than in girls. Girls are likely to be just as troubled by marital turmoil as boys. But they may demonstrate their feelings in a manner more appropriate to their sex role, by becoming withdrawn, for example. The age of a child did not appear to be an important determinant on the effects of marital turmoil. An especially warm relationship with at least one parent can mitigate, though not eliminate, the effects of marital turmoil on children. There was some evidence that changes in discipline as a result of divorce led children, boys especially, to be less compliant with parental commands than children in intact families. Emery summarized that parents involved in conflict with each other are probably poorer role models, more inconsistent with their discipline and placed more stress on their children.

Camara and Resnick (1989) studied a sample of eighty-two families, including divorced and two-parent families.[20] The study used a composite of inter-parental conflict made up of seven ratings: the degree of positive affect expressed by the father towards the mother, the degree of positive affect expressed by the mother towards the father, the degree of negative affect expressed by the father towards the mother, the degree of negative affect expressed by the mother towards the father, the degree of hostility and anger in the home, the extent to which conversations between parents were stressful or tense, and the degree of both overt and subtle conflict in the relationship. Even three years after the separation of the parents, there were significant differences in social behaviour among groups. Children from divorced families showed the highest levels of aggression and behavioural problems and the lowest levels of pro-social behaviour and general self-esteem. However, the results for both divorced and non-divorced families regarding conflict resolution were similar. Parents who reported their spouses using verbal attack, avoidance or physical anger in resolving disagreements tended to have lower levels of cooperation and higher levels of conflict. The outcome of disagreements was more likely to result in an escalated conflict. Parents who were able to reach a compromise in resolving conflicts were more likely to cooperate on parental issues. Therefore, regardless of the level of conflict between the spouses, cooperation between the adults in their parental roles was associated with closer, warmer and more communicative relationships. This could be between children and their non-custodial parent in divorced families, and between children and their mothers in non-divorced families.

Morrison and Coiro (1999) examined two hypotheses. Do children of highly conflicted parents who divorce exhibit a decrease in behavioural problems, while children of low-conflict parents who divorce exhibit an increase in behavioural problems? And do children whose high-conflict families remain together show increased behavioural problems than those whose parent's divorce? The authors used a sample of 727 children from data in the National Longitudinal Survey of Children and Youth (NLSCY). They used responses about the frequency that a spouse argued about nine topics, such as children, money, chores and responsibilities. They found that prior reports with high levels of marital conflict had a large and statistically significant adverse effect on children's behavioural problems. Indeed, the adverse effect of frequent marital quarrels was greater than the deleterious effect of separation and divorce. However, there was no indication of a benefit to the children who left high-conflict families.

Furthermore, the greatest increase in behavioural problems was observed among children whose parents remained married despite frequent quarrels and conflicts.

In the section below (and chapters thereafter), I present an analysis of the married life of Satyavati and Shantanu (and others in the lineage) using several instances presented in the Mahabharata. The marital dyad analysis should give us some idea whether the quality of the relationship between them had any effect on their children's personality and behaviour.

The First Couple in the Lineage

There isn't much literature describing the dynamic of Satyavati and Shantanu's relationship because the latter died soon after their two sons were born. C.G. Jung, while outlining the characteristics of the maiden or 'kanya', describes her 'as not altogether human in the usual sense; she is either of unknown or peculiar origin, or she looks strange or undergoes strange experiences'[21] (Jung C., 1991) If at that time a woman was satisfied with her identity as a man's personal property and nothing else, then she lacked individuality in the society and was projected as a symbol of his masculinity. However, it can also be concluded that the maiden took advantage of the 'anima of man' to further her own interests. Therefore, in spite of the categorization and marginalization, the maidens were comfortable accepting blame as well as appreciation.[22] (Jung C., 1991) According to Pradeep Bhattacharya, the anima is characterized by 'a secret knowledge, a hidden wisdom . . . something like a hidden purpose, a superior knowledge of life's laws[23] (Bhattacharya, 2004), which we can witness in a group of women in the epic. Just like Bhishma, Dhritarashtra, Pandu, the Kaunteyas, and Sugriva, Shantanu could never be disinterested in Satyavati and was always in awe of her.[24] (Bhattacharya, *Five Holy Virgins, Five Sacred Myths, Living by Their Own Norms* 2017)

Men's fascination for women is evident by the attention they pay in defending themselves against their natural affinity. They muse about women as a subgroup and devise rules about their behaviour towards them. The reverse is not recorded in the Mahabharata and we do not have women's insights into the nature of men.[25]

In his work, Narendra Kohli describes the conversation that takes place between Satyavati and Shantanu after she first comes to live at the palace.[26] The conversation points out the awkwardness that both of them felt about the marriage. Satyavati still seemed to be in love with sage Parashara, and hence was uncomfortable when Shantanu tried to reach out to her. Kohli present several other instances that indicate consistent lack of understanding and mutuality throughout their married life.

As I have mentioned earlier, she did not send Vichitravirya and Chitrangada to gurukul to pursue formal education due to her insecurities about Bhishma.[27] Shantanu's reluctance to allow this showed that there was lack of understanding and intellectual balance between husband and wife in the marriage. Shantanu knew it was difficult to argue with Satyavati and instill sense in her. She was happy with the fulfillment of her own self-interests. He also knew that he would not be able to live peacefully if Satyavati grew indifferent to him. When he tries to make her understand the importance of learning at a gurukul under a guru's supervision, she discards his views stating that it is more important to gain knowledge than to understand the needs and emotions of the guru, and knowledge can be gained at home as well. She says that for her, it is more important that her sons realize that they are the masters and the guru is just a royal servant. According to her, this attitude would be beneficial for her sons as rulers. Even though it would make them arrogant and aggressive. As mentioned before, she also refused to let Bhishma be her sons' teacher on the pretext that he might take revenge by harming them and teaching them qualities that they should not learn as princes, such as selflessness, spirituality and humbleness. Here again, Satyavati's insecurity and envy towards Bhishma is evident.

Shantanu asked her what kind of a woman she was, devoid of motherly instinct, sensitivity and generosity. She replied by saying that she was a woman who liked materialistic things.[28] She equated herself to mother earth who has the desire to enjoy everything in nature. Likewise, Kohli's Satyavati desires to enjoy and have rights over wealth, prosperity and politics. She dislikes anything related to spirituality, sacrifice and selflessness, and wishes the same for her sons. These characteristics of Satyavati are negative in every sense. At this instance, Shantanu repented marrying her. This discord between husband and wife shows how dissatisfied they were when it came to marital bliss. He even contemplated abandoning her or leaving the palace himself.[29] But he feared she would tarnish his image by lying about him. If she gained the trust of his subjects and blamed him for her misery, she could give the Kuru dynasty a bad name. In order to avoid this situation, Shantanu put up with Satyavati and never went against her wishes.[30] He even suggested that Bhishma should forcefully take over the kingdom, as he was the best king Hastinapur could get. Otherwise, his other sons along with their mother would destroy the kingdom with their greed for power and wealth.

If we look at contemporary literature to analyse the dynamics of their relationship, it is easy to assume that they were happily married at the outset but difficult to ascertain whether they were actually satisfied later in their lives. In literature, a robust correlation is found between marital quality and personality traits. Personality plays an important role in a relationship, beginning with the selection of one's partner, to the way the partners perceive, communicate with, and behave towards one another.[31] (Vollrath et al, 2010) The psychological approach focuses on the predictive power of stable, personal characteristics in explaining marital satisfaction. And as a consequence, the risk of divorce in current times has increased relatively. If we apply the same approach in the era of the Mahabharata, where divorce was not a known concept, we can easily imply that dissatisfaction in marriage can lead to separation or abandonment. Then why did Shantanu and Satyavati stay together till he died? Was it a compromise on both sides, where Shantanu's lust was satisfied upon fulfillment of Satyavati's wishes (despite his affection for his son Bhishma who suffered injustice due to Satyavati's unfair demands)? Or was there a social stigma involved as a consequence of their separation?

A greater proportion of a woman's life is family-related. Her interests and activities tend to be more family-centred than her husband's. Since our culture tends to define her role as revolving around her family, there may be greater pressure on her to develop an accommodative attitude in relation to other members of the family.[32] (Siriamaki, 1948) In this case, Satyavati was doing the same thing when it came to differentiating between her husbands and sons. Therefore, a difference in the understanding of their duties may detract from marital satisfaction if two married partners have widely differing expectations from the roles of husband and wife. Such disputes can lead to poor psychological development of their children.

Such was the case of Chitrangada and Vichitravirya. They grew up to be pampered, disrespectful, arrogant and psychologically ill. Such children may grow up with the idea that one parent is at fault and the other deserves hatred for the wrongs committed towards the other. This can result in an unhealthy relationship between the parent and the children as well. It may lead to adjustment issues along with symptoms of psychological problems.[33] (Kelly, 2000) Also, children who witness marital disputes in their family tend to be hostile towards the institution of marriage as they never had a good example at home to look up to.[34] (Burman, 1995) The risk of child psychopathology is even greater among children who are exposed to stressful lives of their parents. The adverse effects of that on the development of children's behavioural or emotional problems are prevalent.[35] (Conger, 1997).

This shows how two individuals, with prominent negative personality traits come together in a marriage. And what the outcome of such a union can be.

References

Camara, K., and G. Resnick. (1989). Styles of Conflict Resolution and Cooperation Between Divorced Parents: Effects on Child Behavior and Adjustment. *American Journal of Orthopsychiatry* 59(4): 556–75.

Cowan, P.A., and Cowan, C.P. (2002). Interventions as Tests of Family Systems Theories: Marital and Family Relationships in Children's Development and Psychopathology. *Development and Psychopathology* 14: 731–59.

Cummings, E., and Davies, P.T. (2010). *Marital Conflict and Children: An Emotional Security Perspective*. New York: Guilford.

Davies, P.T., and Cummings, E.M. (1994). Marital Conflict and Child Adjustment: An Emotional Security Hypothesis. *Psychological Bulletin* 116: 387.

Emery, R.E. (1982). Interparental Conflict and the Children of Discord and Divorce. *Psychological Bulletin* 92(2): 310.

Erel, O., and Burman, B. (1995). Interrelatedness of Marital Relationship and Parent-Child Relations: A Meta-Analytic Review. *Psychological Bulletin* 118(1): 108.

Grych, J.H., and Fincham, F.D. (1990). Marital Conflict and Children's Adjustment: A Cognitive-Contextual Framework. *Psychological Bulletin* 108: 267.

Harold, G.T., and Conger, R.D. (1997). Marital Conflict and Adolescent Distress: The Role of Adolescent Awareness. *Child Development* 68: 330.

Rhoades, K.A. (2008). Children's Responses to Inter-Parental Conflict: A Meta-Analysis of Their Associations with Child Adjustment. *Child Development* 79: 1942.

Towle, C. (1931). The Evaluation and Management of Marital Status in Foster Homes. *American Journal of Orthopsychiatry* 1: 271.

Zimet, D.M., and Jacob, T. (2001). Influences of Marital Conflict on Child Adjustment: Review of Theory and Research. *Clinical Child and Family Psychology Review* 4(4): 319.

2

AMBIKA AND AMBALIKA

The Reluctant Wives and Mothers

Not much is found about Ambika and Ambalika in the epic, since their role is insignificant and limited. Nonetheless, they are critical to our inquiry as the mothers of two important characters, Dhritarashtra (son of Ambika) and Pandu (son of Ambalika). It is important to know the personality dispositions of Ambika and Ambalika to see if their traits are transmitted to their sons.

A swayamvara was organized by the king of Kashi for his three daughters, Amba, Ambika and Ambalika. During the swayamvara, all three were taken by force by Bhishma after he challenged and defeated the assembled kings and princes. He presented the princesses to Satyavati, for marriage to Vichitravirya. Vichitravirya married both Ambika and Ambalika. Amba was freed to go her way after she expressed her reluctance to marry Vichitravirya because she had already accepted King Salva as her husband before the swayamvara. Therefore, Bhishma let her go. As interesting as Amba's story may be, we do not need to venture into it since she did not add to the lineage of the Kuru dynasty.

In the Mahabharata, the power of force and abduction was more prized than the sacred ceremonies of a swayamvara. During the swayamvara of Amba, Ambika and Ambalika, Bhishma said:

> Sages have said that, that wife is dearly to be prized who is taken away by force, after the slaughter of opponents, from amidst the concourse of princes and kings invited to a self-choice ceremony.[1] (Book 1: Sambhava Parva 219)

This gives the message that a woman who is abducted or taken by force or through the killing of other opponents is the most-valued possession for a man. So, we see that the entire cultural idea of swayamvara as an emancipation of women's consent may be overrated. This practice actually validates violence and killing. This social practice is an example of an instance when males failed to dominate the opposite sex. This is why they had to rely on force and violation. Use of force was a strong patriarchal practice, which ensured complete submission from women like Ambika and Ambalika. In such circumstances, it can be said that Ambika and Ambalika never got to express their wills and were always suppressed. Their personalities resembles individuals exhibiting neurotic tendencies more than any other negative personality trait.

The abduction of these three sisters by the authoritative Bhishma foregrounds the principle of patriarchal authority. This incident is important in terms of independent choice and the question of consent. These three women were deprived of both at the time. Bhishma abducted all three sisters from their swayamvara so that Vichitravirya could marry them. The noticeable fact here is that the sisters were not abducted by their future husband, Vichitravirya, but by his half-brother. Also, whether they agreed to marry him or were forced to marry him is unrecorded. Moreover, despite being the prince of Hastinapur, Vichitravirya was just a child. He was not mature enough to fulfill the duties of a husband. Ambika and Ambalika were married to him because they were won by Bhishma and no other man would accept them due to that. This shows how helpless they were. This marriage was imposed on them without their will. Vichitravirya did not have the same calibre as his brother Bhishma or the other princes attending the ceremony. But he still possessed the sisters as they were won for him. The princesses were treated like objects and nobody questioned his authority over them. Although young, Ambika and Ambalika were still older than Vichitravirya. They felt helpless and unhappy in this marriage, with no choice but to obey their abductor, and their immature and unworthy husband. They were depressed and melancholic. This eventually led to anxiety and nervousness. These traits are widely acknowledged under neuroticism in personality. Perhaps this was the reason behind their sudden emotional instability or expression of horror when they saw Veda Vyasa in their chambers while submitting themselves to the tradition of *niyoga*.

Various evidence in different works on the Mahabharata, including Kohli's literature, suggest that Vichitravirya possessed some unhealthy habits, such as alcoholism. However, Satyavati was determined to see a great line of kings coming from him. She waited in anticipation for the birth of an heir. Even though Vichitravirya was forbidden to have alcohol and sexual intercourse due to his poor health and young age, he continued to do so. Eventually, he developed tuberculosis and died. Therefore, Ambika and Ambalika were not only deprived of marrying men of their choice, but also of a happy married life.

As per the Manu Dharma Sastram (applicable to the Treta Yuga and Dwapara Yuga), if a woman was widowed without having any sons she could have a son through her dead husband's brother. This was the system of *niyoga*. So, when Vichitravirya died without any sons, his mother Satyavati approached Vichitravirya's half-brother to cohabit with Ambalika and Ambika to bless them each with a son. Bhishma refused on account of his vow of celibacy. Then she asked her own son Veda Vyasa and he obliged. It is very clear that in this case Ambika and Ambalika were obedient but unhappy to go through with this process.[2] It was also legal for a man to approach a Brahman or a deva to give him a son through his wife during those times.[3]

When Vyasa visited Ambika, she saw his dreadful, unkempt appearance and burning eyes. In her frightened state, she closed her eyes during the intercourse. Hence, her son Dhritarashtra, the father of the Kauravas, was born blind. In a few versions of the Mahabharata, Ambika is shown to have no strong motherly feelings towards her blind son Dhritarashtra as he was unwanted. Here again, the decisions of the elders were imposed on her sister and her without their permission. Similarly, when Vyasa visited Ambalika she got frightened and became pale during the intercourse. Hence, her son Pandu, the father of the Pandavas, was born pale and weak. Neuroticism signifies the tendency to experience negative effects such as nervousness, depression and fear. It also involves behaviours such as lack of self-acceptance, lack of self-control and a poor ability to manage psychological stress and emotional stability. All of these affects were visible in Ambika and Ambalika who had submitted themselves to their fates in the hands of the Kuru clan.

After Dhritarashtra's birth, Satyavati requested Vyasa to visit Ambika for a second time. She dared not go and sent her maid instead. The maid also bore a son, Vidura, who was raised as a brother of Dhritarashtra and Pandu.

In the Mahabharata, women's sexuality and sexual relations are dominated by both men and women. When Vichitravirya died without leaving behind an heir, Satyavati took the responsibility of giving an heir to the Kuru dynasty. She did not even inform her daughters-in-law about Vyasa. Instead she just ordered Vyasa and sent him to their chambers. This resulted in unwanted reactions from the two sisters, which bore negative impacts on their sons. These incidents highlight the unhappiness, reluctance and helpless obedience of Ambika and Ambalika due to their marriage to Vichitravirya that was forced upon them. They seem to exhibit neurotic personalities characterized by persistent worrying and anxiety. A person may experience stress as a result of events that are beyond their control, as in this case of Ambika and Ambalika. Neuroticism can also lead an individual to dwell on the negative aspects of a situation, rather than the positives as mentioned earlier. That might be the reason why the two did not raise their voices along with Amba to show their disagreement over their abduction. Rather, they accepted it as their fate and did not resist, even though they remained unhappy and dissatisfied their entire lives.

III

KAURAVAS

DNA Preservers

1

THE DYAD

Gandhari and Dhritarashtra

Gandhari: The Blind Mother

Marriage as a social institution plays an essential role in the Mahabharata. The ancestry of royal families lends an even greater significance to it. The main objective of marriage has been to keep the chain of procreation unbroken by producing future generations. The institution of marriage has been vital to keep ethical and moral societal protocols prevalent within a confined sexual union. In fact, marriage and *stree*-dharma are interrelated. The analysis of stree-dharma from a matrimonial point of view is necessary in the case of the Mahabharata.[1] We will analyse this here, in the context of Gandhari and Dhritarashtra.[2]

In the case of Gandhari's marriage, the aspect of consent, just like in the case of Amba, Ambika and Ambalika, was missing. Hers is another example of confinement in the epic. The moment Bhishma heard about her boon of begetting a hundred sons, he could not look at her as anything else but the provider of heirs to the Kuru dynasty. She was immediately thought of as a suitable bride for Dhritarashtra. Vyasa wrote,

> Soon after Bhishma heard from the Brahmanas that Gandhari, the amiable daughter of Subala, having worshipped Hara (Shiva) had obtained from the deity the boon that she should have a century of sons. Bhishma, the grandfather of the Kurus, having heard this, sent messengers unto the king of Gandhara [sic] (Book 1: Sambhava Parva 236).[3]

For Bhishma, the most critical issue was to secure the Kaurava lineage. And the most ideal approach to do that was to wed one of the Kaurava princes to Gandhari. Initially, Gandhari's parents were not ready for the marriage due to Dhritarashtra's visual impairment, though later on she was offered to Dhritarashtra. The point to note is that she was not once asked for her consent to wed Dhritarashtra.

The first instance that lays down Gandhari's personality traits is when she gets to know her future husband is blind. She decides to blindfold herself to show respect and compassion towards her significant other. Her father Subala, the ruler of Gandhara, was coerced by the fearsome warlord Bhishma into giving her away in marriage to a prince of a distant land.[4] Despite the fact that she was beautiful and worthy, she didn't question her parents' decision and surrendered herself to her visually impaired spouse. However, she took a pledge to parallel her husband's visual deficiency. So, she covered her own eyes with a piece cloth. Therefore, this woman deprived herself of vision and concealed herself from everyone. Her blindness is symbolic. It is as if she were mocking all the others for overlooking her identity as an individual with rights. This shows her sense of superiority, and excessive need for admiration and attention towards her condition.

While searching for any covert motive of Gandhari in blindfolding herself, I came across an article where the author believed that this action of hers could have been fueled by more than just devotion.[5] This can, in fact, be treated as a valid example of narcissism. Some say Gandhari's voluntary blindfolding was an act of protest and a rebellion against the injustice meted out to her. She was forced to marry a blind man much against her will. Her pride as a woman was hurt and violated. She chose to register her protest in a manner that no other woman had done in the past. She inflicted upon herself the very injustice she rebelled against. It was her way of saying: if they thought that a blind husband was fine for me, then a blindfolded wife is good enough for him. This reveals a side of her character that one does not often come across in the epic. This spotlights her indomitable will to be righteous and moral, and her ability to stand alone and take swift, agonizing decisions, unmindful of the consequences.

Manita Kahlon describes this as a 'silent but a strong protest in opposition to the power games and the forced marriage.'[6] Gandhari's blindfold pointed to the fact that women could not have any opinions or desires. They had to prioritize obligation over desire. The covert choice of a blindfold was a symbol of the injustice done to her and thus the anger because of that injustice.[7] Despite being an intelligent and beautiful girl of a well-known dynasty, Gandhari was married off to a person who was inferior to her in terms of wit. Her wit was evident from the suggestions she gave to Dhritarashtra about controlling their sons. She also advised Duryodhana to give the Pandavas their share of the kingdom and not engage them in a war. She was well aware that the result would not favour the Kauravas, as the righteousness of the Pandavas would be their strength.

Today Gandhari may be remembered as women whose aim is to love their husbands, and be physically and emotionally available to them. However, have we found Gandhari to be really submissive to her blind husband who was, literally and metaphorically, blind to all the unethical deeds of his sons? Her internal eyes, behind the blindfolded ones, appear to have created an uncommon energy of seeing even what typical visual perception couldn't identify.

The second behavioural instance of her traits was when she repeatedly pleaded with her husband not to deprive the Pandavas[8] of their legitimate share. The thrust of her argument was that Dhritarashtra was first the king and then a father. So, he should be guided in all his decisions by law and the welfare of the people of Hastinapur. Not by his sentiments and ambitions as the father of Duryodhana. In the Kaurava family, we don't see Dhritarashtra conducting himself as a capable father figure. The main individual who was bold enough to call attention to the Kaurava's wrongdoings was their mother. Gandhari's assertiveness and excessive need for admiration from others around her imply her strong feelings of equity and morality. Her idea of righteousness was so strong and profound that it became a part of her identity. And therefore, she thought that everyone else was inferior to her in being righteous.

The third instance depicting her personality traits in Ganguli's translation of the Mahabharata is as follows:

Sometime after Gandhari conceived and she bore the burden in her womb for two long years without being delivered. And she was greatly afflicted at this. It was then that she heard that Kunti had brought forth a son whose splendour was like unto the morning sun. Impatient of the period of gestation which had prolonged so long, and deprived of reason by grief, she struck her womb with great violence without the knowledge of her husband. And thereupon came out of her womb, after two years' growth, a hard mass of flesh like unto an iron ball. When she was about to throw it away, Dwaipayana, learning everything by his spiritual powers, promptly came there, and that first of ascetics beholding that ball of flesh, addressed the daughter of Subala thus, 'What hast thou done?' Gandhari, without endeavouring to disguise her feelings, addressed the rishi and said, 'Having heard that Kunti had brought forth a son like unto *Surya* in splendour, I struck in grief at my womb.'

In these lines, Gandhari's envy and desire to be the mother of the heir to the throne is so prominent. One can easily see her narcissistic and neurotic character. She is only concerned about her stature as the 'rajmata', and maintaining her superiority over Kunti in the palace.

The fourth instance that highlights her personality was when Duryodhana came and asked her for the boon of victory in the war. All she said was that victory would be given to those who have been righteous. She knew very well that the Pandavas were righteous, and that was their strength in the war. Due to her need to feel superior, she could not give the boon of victory to her son. However, she was also a mother. So, she asked Duryodhana to come naked when she opened her blindfold for the first time since she had put it on. Her eyes had powerful energy, which could convert his mortal body to a body as hard as iron. This would make him invincible in war. She was emotionally unstable, and unable to choose between her role as a mother and as a righteous woman. All of these behavioural instances denote that Gandhari certainly possessed several negative personality traits such as narcissism, psychopathy and Machiavellianism.

Dhritarashtra: The Blind Father

Dhritarashtra, the visually impaired lord, was a physically and ethically blind individual. He does nothing to control his errant children, redressing their acts while Gandhari stays steadfast in her position. He could be seen as a person exhibiting sadistic traits with low self-esteem. Dhritarashtra persisted in acts that prompted disaster since he had a twisted idea of his character. He equated it with worldly desires and belongings. He displayed the kind of shrewd and indecent manners of thinking that are symptomatic of narcissistic, sadistic, and psychotic personality traits. He represents narcissistic, childish individuals who are fanatically distracted with limited feelings of 'I' and 'mine'.

Many scholars believe that the Mahabharata was written in a period when monarchy as an institution was still being established. The question of who should be the successor was mootable.[9] Another group considers disability as a flaw and deficit. This attitude is deep-rooted; its traces can be found in traditional texts, scriptures and even social narratives. Dhritarashtra, the oldest, blind son of King Vichitravirya, is deprived of being crowned king as is customary after the father's death. Visually impaired, he is perceived as deficient and thus not competent enough to be the ruler. Instead his younger brother Pandu, who is not disabled, is nominated as the king. When Pandu dies, Dhritarashtra is appointed as the ruler. However, that is to be only until Pandu's sons are old enough to rule the kingdom. This is ironical, as when there is absolutely no choice, Dhritarashtra's impairment ceases to matter. Dhritarashtra was unable to fight this oppression and his aspirations to acquire what he rightfully considers 'his' royal claim to kingship were in vain. Conventional interpretation paints Duryodhana as the evil-hearted person responsible for perpetuating the final war.

What gets overshadowed is the internalization and transfer, both at a conscious and unconscious level, of the pain, hurt, and anger experienced by a man who is stigmatized for his blindness. One whose psyche is imbalanced because of an absence of moral courage is capable of resorting to brute force to help his cause. However, he can never stay in peace and bliss.[10] Dhritarashtra could never make sense of his identity as ruler or a father, and could never differentiate between these roles. The outcome was the ghastly war, as well as the loss of his descendants, whom he upheld all his life through activities that were unequivocally untrustworthy.

The first instance that points to his negative personality traits was his constant support of his sons' claim to the throne. He refused to give any share to the Pandavas, even when he knew it was wrong. Guardians play a noteworthy part in moulding the lives of their kids, and Dhritarashtra's children too followed in the strides of their unjust father. When guardians are avaricious, pretentious, scheming and unjust, their children unknowingly acquire similar attributes.[11] The wretchedness endures in our culture in light of the fact that parents don't understand that children brought up in an unhealthy environment will likewise wind up to be unworthy and unjust. Thus, a king or a leader ought to be honourable and an example to look up to. Dhritarashtra is the exact opposite of this.[12]

The second instance was of him showing outward happiness at the construction of Khandavaprastha from scratch, as it was built into a beautiful kingdom by the Pandavas. But in fact, he shared Duryodhana's jealousy over the development of a new capital. Duryodhana was now hell-bent on acquiring this newly built kingdom, and with his uncle Shakuni, he devised a plan to invite Yudhishthira for a game of dice. It was clear that this was not meant to be a friendly game. Some great deceptions were going to take place. Both Bhishma and Vidura advised Dhritarashtra against sending the invitation (which had to go in Dhritarashtra's name). Dhritarashtra openly expressed his unwillingness to go against Duryodhana's wishes. In a court presided by him, Dhritarashtra watched (or rather heard) with pleasure as Duryodhana won the game, round after round, while the Pandavas lost everything. Cheating was evident but no one said anything. Dhritarashtra, as Duryodhana's father and the king, could have stopped the game, but he did not.

The third behavioural instance demonstrating his traits was when things got out of control during the game of dice. Yudhishthira wagered Draupadi as his last remaining 'possession'. Dhritarashtra said and did nothing at this blatant violation of a woman's basic right to be free. Even when Draupadi was being stripped, he remained silent. It seemed all his sense of raj-dharma, and even plain decency, had left him. By the time he paid heed to her helpless pleadings and called for a halt, it was too late. The three boons offered to Draupadi could not make up for all that had transpired thus far.

The fourth instance was at the end of the Pandavas' exile, when they came to claim their kingdom. Krishna came as an emissary of the Pandavas, not so much to enforce the agreement, but to negotiate a settlement. He pleaded for five villages or even five houses for the Pandavas to live in. Duryodhana refused to give them anything. And Dhritarashtra did nothing. War could have been averted at this stage if he had exerted his authority, but he failed to do so. Unlike Bhishma, Dhritarashtra had full positional power being the king. The duties as a king ought to have taken precedence over his duties as a father, especially when his son was so plainly jealous, unscrupulous and unfair. It is an ethical imperative to do one's duty. Favouritism ultimately exacts its price. Thus, he failed both the moral and the ethical test. His actions can't be justified even from a consequentialist point of view. For that, the overall welfare of his kingdom should have been his objective. Instead, he only focused on the welfare of his children. The disastrous consequences emphasized his narcissism, which went to such extremes that it became psychotic in nature.

Gandhari and Dhritarashtra: A Blind Couple

When the Kurukshetra war finally saw the demise of 'adharma' and the inevitable victory of 'dharma', Gandhari went to the jungles along with her husband, Kunti, and Vidura. Once, while roaming around the breathtakingly beautiful Himalayas, which can bring peace even to the most disturbed mind, Gandhari let out a deep sigh. Dhritarashtra realized that his wife was missing her childhood (as Qandahar or Gandhar is also a mountainous region), and was lamenting her married life that had deprived her of the beauty, charm and peace of her pre-marital life. He accused Gandhari of holding this grudge against her parents and her in-laws till the end of her life, when she had nothing more to lose. He further said 'it is true that great injustice was done to you by getting you married to a blind, but have you also not been unjust to me by remaining hurt and unhappy till this day?'

Iravati Karve in Yuganta narrates this conversation between Gandhari and Dhritarashtra, which depicts the dynamics of their relationship as a married couple. Dhritarashtra asks Gandhari with pity, 'Really, Gandhari, your life was ruined by being bound to a blind man, wasn't it? All your life you must have yearned for your parents' home.' Gandhari answered, 'Not at all. The day I married you I suppressed all thoughts of my parents' home. Today I was recalling the country of Gandhara, not the people.

Your Majesty knows that though I lived in the same courtyard as my brother, I never spoke to him.'[13] It was now Dhritarashtra's turn to speak. The scorn was gone from his voice. Almost pleadingly, he said, 'You were deceived. Without being told of my blindness you were married to me. We did you a thousand wrongs, Gandhari. But you have paid them back. Can't you ever forgive and forget?'[14]

When Kunti and Vidura stood up to leave them alone to give them privacy, Dhritarashtra ordered them to stay. He says that so far in their relationship as husband and wife, nothing has been private anyway. So, there was no point in giving them privacy now. As soon as he heard the two sit down, he turned again to Gandhari and said in a choked, excited voice, 'Really, you have punished me severely, Gandhari. I didn't think so at first; at the wedding ritual when you stood with your eyes blindfolded, I did not take it too seriously. I thought that I would plead with you and be able to extinguish your anger with my love. But that was not to be. At night when you came to the bedchamber, your eyes were still bound, and you came stumbling, clutching someone's hand. I was born blind. I had become used to moving about without seeing. But you had deliberately covered your eyes. Your body was not used to blindness. What a horrible night! I don't know why I didn't kill you right then.'[15] The angst and frustration are clear in his words. He regretted her decision to blindfold herself and thought of it as a mockery of his own disability. Gandhari was curt in her reply, and said that he should have killed her then and there in order to avoid such a horrible future. Dhritarashtra passionately asks her not to say such words, as no matter what the present conditions were, the Kuru men will always be Kshatriyas and would never kill a woman. This shows his hypocrisy as he did not raise his voice against Draupadi's disrobing in his court, but now claims that he would never harm a woman. A group of Kshatriyas found honour in disgracing a vulnerable woman in public, but were against killing women. This depicts his narcissistic attitude.

He further goes on to say that he was the king and could have easily torn off her blindfold. But he thought that instead of forcing his decision on her, he would be able to convince her to take it off herself. However, he found her initial resentment become permanent over time. He wished to ask her to take off her blindfold when their children were born, but by that time his heart too had become stoic and devoid of empathy. This indicates his narcissistic and sadistic traits again. He reckons that maybe she would have actually done it not for him, who gave her the opportunity to express herself freely. He further admits that he felt a kind of revengeful pleasure in knowing that she would never see the face of their children.[16] He realized that Gandhari was a devoted wife and would never take her blindfold off because of her strong determination. That is until and unless he ordered her to do so, which he deliberately did not. He questions whose fault it was that Pandu and him had to lead such meaningless lives, indicating his neurotic traits. Was it the suffering and misery that their mothers had to endure, which ultimately decided their fate?

He asks Gandhari if she feels cheated and deceived. He asks for her forgiveness, and also to give up her fight against the unfairness of her life. This implies that he thought she needed to let go of her anger, not only against him but against life itself. He tells her that he may have done injustice to her, but that did not give her the right to do injustice to their children and her entire life. He requests her to finally take off her blindfold, and look at the world and all its beings as they are. She does so, only to give up her life in the forest fire. Her husband, Vidura and Kunti follow suit soon after.

This whole conversation draws a sketch of their married life. Not only were they dissatisfied in their marriage, but also with themselves and their lives. The manner in which she expressed her empathy with her blind husband was indeed extraordinary. Of her own accord, she chose to be sightless as her husband. She lived as a blind woman for the rest of her long and tortured life, sharing the pain, prejudices and darkness of her husband. It was indeed an enormous sacrifice. The question, however, is whether it was an act of intense love for her husband or her way of rebelling against the blind society that ruined her life. I believe it was not her way of showing solidarity to her husband, but a way of reminding him of all the wrongdoings of the Kuru men that had deprived her of her rights and pleasures.

In either case, it meant that she was now as disabled and helpless as her husband. Both of them were unable to help, guide or support the other. And both had to depend on external help. Therefore, by necessity, there always had to be a third person in their married life. Surely, this was not the best way to be husband and wife, especially when other choices were available.

Through these instances it can be inferred that when a person with negative personality traits like narcissism, psychopathy, neuroticism and sadism marries another person with negative personality traits, the consequences can be disastrous.

Gandhari, unlike most other women in the epic, was a completely devoted and faithful wife. But her devious husband routinely took palace maids to his bed. There was an inherent strife in their conjugal life. Gandhari was disappointed in love and marriage. Some say she was cold to her husband. Physically, they had to be together by necessity. They had been forced together by a quirk of fate, but also by her self-inflicted punishment. Emotionally, they remained apart. At the very end, it was only the unbearable agony of losing all their sons and grandsons that brought them close.

At the same time, Dhritarashtra himself struggled with many complexes, disappointments and frustrations. He could never come to terms with the bitter fact that his kingship was taken away merely because he was blind. He felt it was totally unjust. He blamed fate and the elders in the family for playing a cruel trick on him. The denial of kingship burnt a searing hole in his heart. The unexpected death of Pandu, his brother, opened his way to the throne. And when Gandhari's womb produced sons, a new ray of hope dawned in Dhritarashtra's heart. He fondly came to believe that his eldest son Duryodhana would rightfully succeed him as the king of Hastinapur. Since he was the king, he strongly believed that his sons should be heirs to the throne. He doted on his eldest son, and supported his cunning schemes, covertly or otherwise. All her life, Gandhari was surrounded by a weak but ambitious husband, a treacherous, scheming brother called Shakuni, and hate-filled, misguided sons. And, none of them paid heed to her words, much less cared for her feelings. Gandhari, the queen, the mother of a hundred sons, was indeed a very lonely woman.

Gandhari helplessly watched her family drift towards self-destruction. She was torn in many directions, by her maternal affections, her duty to her husband and her sense of justice. But her agony, loneliness and predicament were neither shared nor appreciated by her husband. Within her was a simmering volcano of frustration and rage, borne out of a sense of betrayal, pain, loneliness and neglect. Above all, it was fueled by the injustice meted out to her.

Gandhari's act of opting to be sightless raises questions about the essence of married life. Should one attempt to be a replica of his or her spouse? Or should the partners in a marriage mutually complement each other by supporting each other's abilities and try to make up for the other's shortcomings? What is of greater value in a marriage: similarity or compatibility?

When Gandhari blindfolded herself to be sightless like her husband, she became a female counterpart of the blind king. She could have made other choices. She could have tried to be the eyes and wisdom of her husband (since he lacked both). Surely, that would have been more purposeful. Had Gandhari stepped in to administer the kingdom on behalf of the blind king and taken charge of the affairs of the state, the tale of Mahabharata would have been rather different. It would have been more forthright and challenging, since Gandhari was a courageous, ambitious woman with a good heart. But she seemed to have surrendered her initiative too easily and without a thought. She drifted through the vagaries of life blindfolded, helpless and uncared for. Kunti, on the other hand, successfully carried out her duties as both, a matriarch and an assertive wife.

In the end, the gory battle swallowed all of Gandhari's sons. Her pleas to make peace with the Pandavas were ignored by the Kauravas, and her warnings about the fatal prophecy about the ruin of the clan with Duryodhana's birth were dismissed by Dhritarashtra. This is why when Duryodhana came to seek her blessings, she just said 'only where righteousness is, victory be' (Chaitanya 1985, p. 159-63).[17] This statement is an example of profound observation, highlighting an eternal truth as well as an unalterable providence.

The stirring experiences of an engaged reader upon reading the Mahabharata lends significance and vibrancy to the epic poem. These characters show what the consequences of the union of two individuals with negative personality traits can be. This eventually leads to an unsuccessful and dissatisfied married life, and thus troubled offspring.

2

Duryodhana

A Judgemental Assessment

Using the villainous personality traits of Machiavellianism, narcissism, neuroticism, psychopathy and everyday sadism, the current chapter attempts to judge Duryodhana and his misdeeds. In other words, this chapter presents a scientific assessment of the degree to which his personality had these five villainous dispositional characteristics. Thus, we deal in two variables to assess Duryodhana's dispositional characteristics. The five villainous personality traits and Duryodhana's various actions and behaviours.

To assess Duryodhana's personality, I refer to two important research works conducted by social scientists R.J. Deluga (1997)[1] and Arijit Chatterjee and Donald C. Hambrick (2007).[2] Deluga examined the personalities of thirty-nine American presidents, ranging from George Washington to Ronald Reagan, using historiometric methods. Historiometry examines biographical information of historical figures using quantitative measurement, without any prior theoretical commitment. This methodology includes content analysis and the use of adapted personality instruments with biographical works. As such, it attempts to establish personality patterns from the particular to the general across a sample of cases. In historiometry, profiles of subjects are prepared by abstracting personality descriptions verbatim from numerous standard biographical sources and fact books. These profiles are prepared as objectively as possible.

Further, Chatterjee and Hambrick (2007) examined the effects of the personalities of chief executive officers (CEOs) of American computer software and hardware companies on the financial performance of their firms. The researchers used unobtrusive measurements such as the prominence of the CEO's photograph in the company's annual report, the CEO's prominence in the company's press releases, the CEO's use of first-person singular pronouns in interviews and the CEO's cash and non-cash compensation in comparison to other top managers in the firm. Other unobtrusive measures include physical traces (evidence people leave behind in their physical environment), non-participant observation, documentary sources, written and spoken words of subjects, structure of offices and bedrooms, contents of personal web sites and consumption patterns as ways to learn about their preferences, perceptions and personalities.

I employ similar unobtrusive techniques to assess Duryodhana's dispositional characteristics across the five villainous personality dimensions. I will rely on the singular primary source of information—the Mahabharata. Duryodhana is a leading villainous character, so there are sufficient instances to assess him along the five personality dimensions. In the following section, I present several instances from the Mahabharata and map them on to the five personality dimensions.

Dispositional Mapping

Duryodhana is one of the major characters of the Mahabharata. He was the eldest of the Kauravas—the hundred sons of Dhritarashtra and Gandhari. Being the firstborn son of the blind king, he was the crown prince of Hastinapur along with his older cousin Yudhishthira (eldest of the five Pandavas).

When we analyse Duryodhana's characteristics to categorize him according to certain negative personality traits, it is obvious that he was evil right from the start.[3] But what makes Duryodhana an evil person? There is a regular reiteration of offences against the Pandavas by Duryodhana. These include the attempted poisoning and drowning of Bhima, the burning of the 'Laakshyagriha' and all the incidents that took place in the game of dice at the gambling assembly. The memory of the humiliation faced by Draupadi and the whole Pandava family when the menstruating Draupadi is dragged by her hair and clothes, upon Duryodhana's orders, through the 'circle of kings' fueled a want for retaliation in the Pandavas. This is a leading motive till the very end of the war. Draupadi's contempt and Bhima's fury are so powerful that in many places in the Sanskrit Mahabharata, and in various different retellings, Draupadi's insult and its outcome are an indispensable feature of the story. From this point of view, this violation is seen as the main sin of its perpetrator—Duryodhana.

Throughout the epic, Duryodhana is steadfast in his enmity against the Pandavas. We are not suggesting that enmity is a virtue. We are simply bringing notice to the fact that, good or bad, Duryodhana's thoughts, beliefs and actions always fell in a single line. There is not a single instance where he repents or reconsiders his actions. Even as he is dying, he tries to belittle Yudhishthira, laughing at the hollow victory of the Pandavas. He is convinced that he is right in coveting the wealth of the Pandavas. He says with authority, 'Discontent is the root of prosperity. Therefore, O king, I desire to be discontented. He that striveth after the acquisition of prosperity is, O king, a truly politic person.'[4] According to him, it is Kshatriya dharma (the dharma or the duty of the ruler class) to covet the property of others and expand one's territory. So, he is only following this dharma when he schemes to acquire the kingdom of the Pandavas. Duryodhana is defined by the jealousy he harbours for the Pandavas. This characteristic trait is a part of his identity.

Right from the beginning, when Kunti comes back to Hastinapur seeking refuge, Duryodhana is tormented by a feeling of insecurity. He fears the kingdom will go to Yudhishthira, the eldest prince and the son of Pandu. His own father, Dhritarashtra, was only a custodian in the absence of Pandu. The thought of being at the mercy of the Pandavas is so appalling to him that he tries everything in his means to eliminate them. Though Bhima childishly tormented the Kauravas, but never with malice,[5] Duryodhana, already insecure, developed a deep-rooted hatred for Bhima and his brothers.

In the following section, using instance-based historiometry,[6] I present various behavioural instances that throw light on Duryodhana's personality traits. They are also indicative of the degree to which Duryodhana's personality had elements of the five negative personality traits discussed earlier.

Behavioural Instances Indicating Personality Traits in Duryodhana

The first instance that highlights his negative personality traits was also his first act of insolence against the Pandavas in his early days. At the time, the Pandavas and their mother Kunti had come to Hastinapur after Pandu's demise. Yudhishthira was sixteen years old and Duryodhana was a year younger to him. Growing up, Bhima had unparalleled physical power, and used to mock and defeat the Kauravas. Bhima's perky tricks of suffocating them in water, shaking them down the trees and pulling them by hair left Duryodhana outraged. Unfit to counter him alone, Duryodhana resorted to spite and scheming. The plot he considers is pre-planned. The insidiousness of this young boy as he carefully ascertains the pros and cons of his evil plan is shocking. The Pandavas greatly depended on Bhima's prowess. Duryodhana realized that if he succeeded in killing Bhima, he could easily overwhelm and arrest Yudhishthira and then Arjuna. With these three Pandava siblings out of his way, there would be no one to stop him and he would be the heir apparent of Hastinapur.[7] He thoughtfully and painstakingly measures every potential outcome.

He erects a castle in Pramanakoti, on the banks of Ganga. He constructs this royal residence for water sports and then welcomes the Pandavas to join him. When they arrive, all the servants are asked to leave and the princes go around exploring the magnificence of the place. While they are occupied with different games and recreation, Duryodhana treats Bhima to delicious food laced with poison. Bhima eats the food and due to the effects of the poison, becomes unconscious. Thereafter, Duryodhana ties his limbs and drowns him in the river so that all chances of his survival are negated. When Bhima doesn't return in the evening, Yudhishthira and his brothers frantically search for him. Though everybody thinks that Duryodhana was behind this, no one questions him. The authority he impressed upon others, even at that early age, shows the powerful nature of his character. Later, Bhima returns with his strength increased manifold with the blessings of Vasuki, the Naga king. This instance gives one an insight into the cruel and devious mind of Duryodhana.

Through the analysis of these behavioural instances, it seems that Duryodhana had Machiavellian traits in him since his early days. This incident shows how he could go to any extent to safeguard his interests, even if it meant engaging in immoral acts and behaviours. His lack of empathy towards others and the sense of superiority he felt about himself are obvious. This highlights his narcissistic and psychopathic traits, along with the Machiavellian ones. It also shows his neurotic tendencies. His excessive jealousy leads to anxiety and outrage, fueling him to take revenge on the Pandavas.

The second behavioural instance that highlights his negative dispositions was when after being defeated in his first attempt to vanquish the Pandavas, he and his father plan another plot against them. This time Duryodhana did not concentrate on Bhima alone, but on all the five siblings along with their mother, Kunti. After making this plan, he waits for a whole year to execute it. In this time he tries to win over the people of Hastinapur by doing innumerable good deeds and giving away much wealth to the poor and needy. Only after ascertaining that he had earned a good name with the people does he act on his plan. On his instruction, he asks Dhritarashtra to send the Pandavas to the city of Varanavata to witness the merriments there. In Varanavata, the Pandavas stay in a castle constructed exclusively for them. On Duryodhana's command, Purochana has fabricated the palace with lac and other flammable objects. Even after the Pandavas reach Varanavata, Duryodhana does not act immediately. He waits another year. Only after making sure that no one suspects him of harbouring evil intentions does he command Purochana to set fire to the palace of lac. At an ideal moment, when nobody presumes anything, Purochana sets the royal residence ablaze. Thus, hoping to kill the Pandavas and Kunti. We see that the Duryodhana's wrath is of such great magnitude that he isn't ready to spare even Kunti. Of course, with Vidura's timely intervention, the Pandavas escape to safety and survive. This second incident throws light on Duryodhana's sly maturity in executing premeditated evil plans. His emotions against the Pandavas have only grown stronger, but he is not impulsive. He is willing to wait to get the desired results. Every move is well thought out and calculated. This cold bloodedness shows his criminal intent and manipulative character. Along with Machiavellian traits, he also exhibits psychopathic tendencies.

The third instance of his behaviour where he shows psychopathic traits was when he could not win Draupadi's hand in her swayamvara, as he failed to bend the bow to hit the target. Duryodhana's mental make-up was such that he could not stomach failure, and he did not accept this defeat gracefully. Instead, he instigates the other kings to rise against the young 'brahman' Arjuna (in disguise) who had won the contest. His need to always win and feel superior to others is paramount. It becomes psychopathic in nature when he resorts to immoral and criminal acts that harm others.

The fourth instance that exemplify his personality traits to be similar to that of a narcissist is his acts of chivalry that he uses to portray himself as a good person in people's eyes, even though these were driven by his hatred for his cousins. On seeing the valorous young Karna throwing a challenge at Arjuna, only to be rejected as an unequal *suta putra*, he rejects any class difference at birth and declares that only valour will merit honour. Even though borne out of a negative motive, the crowning of Karna by Duryodhana shows him in good light. He is successful in garnering admiration in the hearts of the common public, which could have been his secondary motive.

The fifth instance that indicates his negative disposition was when he expressed his desire to perform the 'rajasuya yajna', just like Yudhishthira had done to establish his prowess in his kingdom and gain the confidence and support of other kings. He requested Veda Vyasa to conduct the rajasuya sacrifice for him in Hastinapur, just like it was done in Indraprastha. But Vyasa declined to do so, citing adharma and evil intention as the reason behind conducting it. Vyasa tells him that the purpose of performing the rajasuya yajna is to establish dharma not to loot the states and force his authority on them. He asked Duryodhana whether he would wash the feet of Lord Krishna, who washed the feet of all the sages present in the rajasuya yajna and proved his humility. Duryodhana refused, and said that he would give donations to all of them but not wash anyone's feet. This depicts his character as one so absorbed in self-love that he refuses to pay respect to Yudhishthira by washing his feet as the host. Vyasa points out that he agrees to donate any amount asked for so that he can boast about it in future and be his arrogant self.[8] Thus, this incident portrayed his narcissistic traits.

The sixth instance that characterizes his negative personality was when he made Karna the commander of his army and sent him on a worldwide military invasion, 'Digvijaya'. Karna embarked upon a worldwide military campaign to subjugate kings and impose Duryodhana's imperial authority over them. Bringing tribute and allegiance from kings all over the world, Karna helped Duryodhana perform the Vaishnava sacrifice to please Lord Vishnu and crown himself 'Emperor of the World', as Yudhishthira had done with the rajasuya. He did this to manipulate the common people into believing that he was the most powerful person in the world. In order to establish that, he used to make daily public announcements of the kingdoms he had won. However, it should be noted that he never mentioned any states that were more powerful than his, and which would be able contenders in warfare. He only mentioned the states that he won against such as Angadesh and Ahikshatra. The common people did not know that these states were already under the territory and authority of Hastinapur. Karna was the ruler of Angadesh and Drona was the head of Ahikshatra, which he seized from Drupada with Hastinapur's support. This information was concealed from the public so that they believed Duryodhana unquestionably. This kind of manipulation to achieve his ends in the competition against the Pandavas again shows Duryodhana's Machiavellian personality traits.

The seventh instance that makes it seem that Duryodhana could have possessed psychopathic traits was when after Yudhishthira's rajasuya yajna, Duryodhana did not leave Indraprastha and stayed in the Pandavas' palace. He was amazed to see the wonderful illusions in the palace built by Mayasura. When Duryodhana tried to enter a door, he hurt his head because it was not really a door but a wall. When he went further, he saw a pool of water and tried to step into it. But it was glass that looked like a pool of water and he hurt his foot on the glass. Bhima and the other Pandavas who were present there were amused and made fun of him when they saw this. Then Duryodhana went ahead and fell into a pool, which looked just like the floor. Seeing this, Draupadi started laughing loudly. She commented, 'A blind man's son is also blind.' This insult hurt Duryodhana so much that he vowed to take his revenge on Draupadi. Duryodhana was jealous of the luxury of the Pandavas' palace. He told his uncle, Shakuni, that he wanted to rob the Pandavas of all the luxury they were enjoying. He wanted it all for himself. Shakuni replied, 'You can't take all this by force. We will take all this from them.' Duryodhana agreed with his uncle and together they started thinking of devious plans to oust the Pandavas from Indraprastha.

The eighth instance that shows his negative personality was the game of dice. It marked the pinnacle of Duryodhana's hatred and insecurity towards the Pandavas. It gives an insight into the appalling dispositions that an individual may have when in the grasp of strong feelings. From here there is no turning back, and Duryodhana proceeds towards his own devastation. This time he goes to considerable lengths to devise a foolproof arrangement, which rules out any positive result for the Pandavas. He realizes that with Drupada and Krishna as allies, it was difficult to defeat them in battle. He also realizes that though Bhishma, Drona, Kripa, Karna and the rest were on his side, the Pandavas were equally powerful and the result of a battle would be unpredictable. With all this in mind, Duryodhana sees the game of dice as the right means to usurp the Pandavas' wealth. There is no bloodshed in the game of dice, and victory is sure. There was no one in the world who could compete with Shakuni in rolling the dice and winning. Though Dhritarashtra was hesitant at first, upon perceiving Duryodhana's affliction, he gave his permission to invite Yudhishthira for the game. Yudhishthira, fully aware that he was no match for Shakuni, accepted the invitation. And the game began. As the momentum picked up, Yudhishthira gradually lost all of his immense wealth. If the game had stopped here, maybe there would have been some redemption for Duryodhana. Although he had gained the entire wealth of the Pandavas, he was not satisfied. Locking arms with Shakuni, he goaded Yudhishthira to play further. Yudhishthira, too caught in the web of desire to win and unable to resist himself, pledged his brothers one by one—Bhima, Arjuna, Nakula, and Sahadeva—and lost all of them. He feverishly played on, even pledging himself. Much to Duryodhana's glee he lost. Yudhishthira, always lauded for fairness of conduct and nobility, stooped to pledging his wife Draupadi. This was an appalling act that would put even the most insolent wretch to shame. As expected, Shakuni won and Draupadi was lost as well. Drunk with the pride of success, and inebriated with his victory over the Pandavas, Duryodhana charted his own doom as he ordered his brother Dusshasana to drag Draupadi to the court. The ever-faithful brother dragged the princess of Panchala to court, seizing her by her hair. Menstruating and attired in a single piece of cloth, Draupadi's piteous requests for decency of conduct fell on deaf ears. Duryodhana's suppressed and hitherto unsatisfied emotions took complete control over him. Unmindful of demeaning himself by insulting the daughter-in-law of the Kuru dynasty, he authorized Dusshasana to disrobe Draupadi in the public court in front of everyone assembled. She was saved by Krishna's divine intervention, miraculously draped with endless yards of cloth, which Dusshasana was not able to remove. However, this dreadful action of disrobing Draupadi sealed Duryodhana's fate as the Pandavas resolved to seek payback for every insult in a befitting manner. Even after this, Duryodhana did not stop his insults. Forgetting that Draupadi was his brother's wife and equivalent to his mother, he moved his garment to reveal his left thigh and taunted Draupadi to come and sit on his lap. There was no stopping him as he heaped insult after insult at the Pandavas and their beloved wife. Nobody except Vidura and Duryodhana's brother Vikarna dared to stop him. It is only then that Dhritarashtra intervened, trying to pacify the Pandavas and Draupadi by reinstating their freedom and returning all the wealth they had lost. Duryodhana was infuriated at Dhritarashtra for letting the

Pandavas go scot-free, and made him bring the Pandavas back for another round of dice. This time he promised that he would not go beyond taking their wealth. The Pandavas came back and Yudhishthira played with the wager that whoever lost would surrender their kingdom and live in exile in the forests for thirteen years. He eventually lost. There was an additional clause, that the thirteenth year should be spent incognito. In case they were identified, they would have to go back to the forest for another thirteen years. The game of dice is an example of the great lengths Duryodhana went to, to exterminate the Pandavas and their mother. This is indicative of the enormity of the psychopathic traits he possessed. He exhibits antisocial behaviour, diminished empathy and remorse, disinhibited or bold behaviour and serious criminal tendencies against the Pandavas. He has psychopathic, Machiavellian, narcissistic and sadistic personality traits. He is disrespectful, particularly with reference to his treatment of Draupadi, and lacks empathy for a woman in vulnerable conditions.

Keeping in mind this last clause of 'agyaatvaas', the ninth instance that makes Duryodhana seem to possess negative personality traits is when he sends spies to the forest in order to track down the Pandavas during the thirteenth year of the exile.[9] The Pandavas were supposed to live in disguise during the thirteenth year of the exile so that nobody could recognize them. If the Kauravas came to know where and in what disguise they were living, the Pandavas would be mandated to spend another twelve years in exile along with another one year of agyaatvaas. Duryodhana wanted to track down the Pandavas and turn their exile into a vicious cycle. He wanted to ensure that they would never return to Hastinapur to claim their kingdom. His cunning plan to deceive the Pandavas and keep the throne for himself shows that Duryodhana was prepared to accomplish the worst possible feat to meet his desired ends. He was also anxious about the outcome if the Pandavas manage to live in agyaatvaas successfully. This is characteristic of an individual who possesses Machiavellian and neurotic traits.

The tenth instance that characterizes his personality traits as narcissistic was when he proved that desires can never be satisfied. He did not stop with sending the Pandavas to the forest. He wanted to see them destitute, gloat in their misfortune, and remind them of all that they had lost to make them more miserable. He confessed to Karna, 'The joy that I may feel in obtaining the sovereignty of the entire earth is nothing to that which will be mine upon beholding the sons of Pandu attired in barks of trees and deer-skins.'[10] On the pretext of supervising the cattle stations, Duryodhana, Karna, Shakuni and others obtained Dhritarashtra's permission and proceeded to the forests. Intoxicated with power, the ever-egoistic Duryodhana commanded his attendants to set up their tents right where the Gandharvas (a sect of celestials) were residing. Annoyed at Duryodhana's interference, the Gandharvas fought the Kaurava army. Unable to withstand the prowess of Chitrasena, the head of the Gandharvas, Karna fled from the battlefield. Duryodhana was held captive. But as fate would have it, Chitrasena happened to be a good friend of Arjuna. On his request, he handed Duryodhana over to Yudhishthira. Yudhishthira set Duryodhana free. As was the tradition, Duryodhana granted Arjuna a boon, which Arjuna later used to his advantage (discussed later in this discourse). How the tables turned. A venture to jeer at the Pandavas ended with Duryodhana bearing the ignominy of being saved and set free by the same Pandavas. His arrogance, a grandiose sense of superiority driven by self-love, his lack of empathy leading to reckless behaviour and the propensity to involve himself in exploitative acts are all indications of his narcissistic and sadistic traits.

Further in this incident, we can see the eleventh behavioural instance. Duryodhana was saved by the Pandavas from the wrath of the Gandharvas in the forest. Instead of being thankful to them, he was disheartened on being saved by his arch enemies. He felt humiliated and thought of giving up his life for the embarrassment he had to face. No love or respect arose in his heart for his saviours. Yudhishthira had asked Arjuna and Bhima to rescue Duryodhana. Duryodhana, being a Kshatriya, granted Arjuna a boon. He would fulfill one of Arjuna's demands anytime in his life. Resolving to die, Duryodhana pledged to fast unto death. He is pacified by Karna, who vows to kill Arjuna in battle and never drink wine until he does so. Duryodhana refused to go back to Hastinapur after being humiliated. He said he would not eat or drink until he died sitting there in the forest. He called Dusshasana, and declared that from thereafter he was relinquishing his kingdom and passing it on to his brother. He did not realize that the kingdom was not his to pass on when he himself was not the king yet! He had cried for the Pandavas to come to his rescue. But after they saved him from Chitrasena he was so humiliated that he felt he should have died on the battlefield rather than being saved by them.[11] This incident shows that Duryodhana considered himself to be so superior to the Pandavas that death was far preferable over being saved by inferior beings. Even though he discontinued his fast after one night saying that the dark forces had urged him not to do so as they were on his side and would help him win, he lacked the dignity to accept his defeat gracefully. Also, the story could have been a mere fabrication to convince people that he lived not because he was afraid to die, but for a higher motive that the dark forces entrusted him with.[12] This, again, showed narcissistic as well as Machiavellian characteristics in his personality.

The twelfth instance that reveals his psychopathic, sadistic traits was when Duryodhana persuaded the sage Durvasa to visit the Pandavas. Durvasa Maharishi was infamous for his temper. Duryodhana slyly appealed to Durvasa to visit the Pandavas with his entire retinue after Draupadi had finished her meal. Surya (the Sun God) had presented the Pandavas with an 'Akshaya Paathra', a vessel that produced endless amounts of food every day until Draupadi had fed all her guests and herself, after which it produced no more food that day. Duryodhana planned for Durvasa to reach the Pandavas' hermitage after everyone had eaten, so there would be no food left. Yudhishthira would be unable to entertain the sage appropriately. Incensed, Durvasa would curse the Pandavas. Of course, with Krishna's timely intervention, the day was saved.[13] (Mahabharata. Vana Parva. 363-1) Duryodhana's jealousy and hatred are at the forefront here. He focuses all his resources on destroying the Pandavas. It is earlier seen that he had the nobility and warm-heartedness that could have earned him respect and recognition on par with that of Yudhishthira. It is sad to note that his emotions constricted him to baseless vengeance. Further, the humiliation that he heaped on the Pandavas, and his inhuman treatment of Draupadi shows us how low an individual can stoop to when his baser instincts get the better of him

Adding to this, the thirteenth instance was when after offering sage Durvasa his hospitality, he sent 9000 soldiers disguised as Durvasa's disciples along with the troupe of a thousand disciples and attendants of the maharishi. He thought that Yudhishthira would not be able to serve a legion of 10,000 people, even if he succeeded in serving the thousand disciples originally accompanying Durvasa.[14] He wanted to ensure that the Pandavas finished all their rations in serving the hungry troupe, and were themselves starved as there would be no food left for them.[15] This lack of empathy and erratic behaviour show that he was, indeed, a psychopath. This cruel motive was foiled by Lord Krishna. And Duryodhana was furious when he came to know that the sage and his troupe did not eat anything at all, leaving immediately after blessing the Pandavas.

The fourteenth instance of his psychopathic behaviour was when Duryodhana sent Jayadratha to kidnap Draupadi while they were staying in an ashram in their thirteenth year of exile.[16] He planned this so that the Pandavas and their entire family would have to come and rescue Draupadi. Their identity would be unveiled as a result of this, and their exile would get extended for another thirteen years.

The fifteenth instance highlights those personality traits of his that resemble Machiavellianism. Duryodhana tricked Shalya, the brother of Madri (mother of Nakula and Sahadeva), into fighting for the Kauravas. He knew very well that Shalya would have supported the Pandavas for their right to the throne.[17] When Shalya came to know of the impending war of Kurukshetra, he marched forth with his army to join his nephews Nakula and Sahadeva. On his way, he was tricked by Duryodhana. He had arranged a magnificent feast for Shalya and his army. Shalya thought that this feast was hosted for him by Yudhishthira and therefore, impressed by Yudhishthira's hospitality, asked to see him and grant him a boon. When Duryodhana revealed the treachery, Shalya was astounded but was compelled to grant a boon as per Kshatriya dharma. Duryodhana asked him to fight for the Kauravas. He resorted to all manners of treachery and manipulation to achieve his self-serving ends. His foremost scheme was to befriend all the enemies of the Pandavas and divide their armies so that they would lose their support from other kingdoms.[18]

The sixteenth instance was when, after the successful completion of one year in hiding, the Pandavas came to Duryodhana and asked for their kingdom, Indraprastha. Duryodhana flatly refused. A priest was sent to the Kauravas asking for their kingdom back to prevent war. Duryodhana ridiculed the priest and sent him back. Then Krishna himself came to the Kauravas and pleaded for at least five villages for the Pandavas, to avoid a war, but Duryodhana did not budge. War was inevitable. Thus started the terrible eighteen-day war between the Kauravas and their allies and the Pandavas and their allies.

During the first ten days of the battle, Bhishma was the general of the Kaurava army. He was the grandfather of both the Pandavas and the Kauravas. Bound by his vow to serve the ruling family of Hastinapur, he fought on the side of the Kauravas. However, Bhishma loved the Pandavas and felt that they were right. Duryodhana knew this and felt that Bhishma, though a fine warrior, was purposely not killing the Pandavas because of his love for them. One night, after a dismal show by the Kauravas in the battle, Duryodhana went to Bhishma and exclaimed that he was ashamed of his fighting. He spoke with undisguised anger, accusing him of fighting on behalf of the Pandavas. Why else was the greatest warrior in the world unable to kill five pathetic humans? Bhishma took a deep breath to calm himself, but he couldn't. Duryodhana's words kept ringing in his head. How could he make Duryodhana believe in him? With great difficulty, Bhishma pulled out five of his arrows. He touched them with his eyes closed. Duryodhana watched this entire scene in bewilderment, wondering what his grandfather was doing. A force left Bhishma's body and entered the five arrows. The five arrows gleamed menacingly. Duryodhana looked at the arrows, afraid to touch them. Bhishma looked weak, the creases on his face were more accentuated than they had been before. He took a deep breath to control himself as he felt his energy draining from him. Bhishma knew what he had done would definitely seal the fate of the Pandavas but as the general of the Kaurava army he had no choice. He was bound to serve his king. He haltingly said that he had put his life force in those arrows. The force in those arrows would not fail. One arrow for each of the Pandavas. Bhishma felt sorry for what he had done. Duryodhana thought that if he left the arrows with Bhishma he might, out of his sense of righteousness, lose them. Or worse, hand them over to the Pandavas. So, he asked Bhishma to give him custody of the five golden arrows, saying that he would return them the next morning. Bhishma tried arguing with Duryodhana but his grandson was adamant and he eventually gave in. Krishna knew that Bhishma had the capacity to make these arrows. He could sense it, and his spies confirmed it. Krishna hurried to Arjuna's camp. He reminded Arjuna of his boon and told him to go to Duryodhana and ask for the five golden arrows. When Arjuna came to ask for the arrows, Duryodhana was shocked and had to comply, being true to his words as a Kshatriya. Duryodhana's distrust and insecurity because of Bhishma's love for the Pandavas eventually led him to lose the only thing that could have won him the war. He provoked Bhishma into creating those arrows because he wanted to kill the Pandavas at any cost. This evil streak in him is additional evidence of his Machiavellian, psychopathic and sadistic traits. He not only wanted his interests to be foremost, but also drew pleasure from the bad fortune and hardships faced by the Pandavas. He went to unparalleled lengths to demean and defeat the Pandavas. He would have even killed them, if not for Krishna, because of his neurotic traits in addition to his other negative personality traits.

The seventeenth instance happened in the Udyoga Parva, during Krishna's visit as the Pandavas' envoy. He requested the Kauravas to give five villages or at least five houses to the Pandavas in Hastinapur. Despite Krishna's recognition as God by everyone around him, Duryodhana's evil self remained unmoved. He refused to see the reality unfolding around him. Fueled by his arrogance and pride, he even attempted to imprison Krishna. Till the very end, the evil forces in Duryodhana remained blind to the supreme God present before them.

The eighteenth instance was when Arjuna and Duryodhana visited Lord Krishna to request his help in their war efforts. This incident shows that even when a choice for redemption is available, the evil mind opts only for lower material benefits. Before the war, Krishna offered both sides to either chose him without arms or his army without him. Arjuna chose the unarmed Krishna while Duryodhana was happy with the Dwaraka army. He did not realize that this army was invincible only because Krishna was its leader. Duryodhana's evil mind was unable to comprehend God's glory, and he choose the material alternative, the army. His narcissism is evident from the air of superiority he does not hesitate to assert, even in front of God.

The nineteenth instance throws light on his narcissistic and neurotic personality traits. When Vidura fed Krishna in his house, Duryodhana flew into a rage and accused him of being a whore's son. This outrage led Vidura to break his bow, which was one of the causes for Duryodhana's defeat. His lack of empathy leading to callousness is prominent in his outrageous behaviour. As is the arrogance and anxiety that fuels his self-destructive course of action.

The twentieth instance depicting his narcissistic nature, was at the end of the war when the Pandavas and Krishna made him an offer—he could pick any of the Pandava brothers to fight against, one-on-one, with a weapon of his choice. If he defeated the Pandava, Duryodhana would be deemed the victor of the war. Duryodhana picked his arch-enemy, Bhima, even though he could have effortlessly overwhelmed the other Pandava brothers with his skill at fighting with the mace. This may seem fair and just. But it may just have been a sense of excessive self-admiration and grandiose self-love where he thought of himself to as superior to all, even Bhima. We cannot negate this possibility, considering that most of his past actions have pointed towards a similar personality trait.

The twenty-first instance showing his psychopathic inclination was when he disregarded battlefield honour after Abhimanyu slayed Duryodhana's son Lakshmana. He commanded all his soldiers to attack Abhimanyu at once. This was foul play from his side. Abhimanyu was the only one who seemed to know how to enter the chakravyuha and destroy it. However, he did not know how to come out of it and Duryodhana knew that. Taking advantage of this knowledge, and Abhimanyu's confusion on being attacked from all sides while he was unarmed inside the chakravyuha, Duryodhana ordered him to be slaughtered.

His deceitful nature continued to prevail until the last hour. He lied to Bhima about where the centre of his life was situated to gain an undue advantage over him in single combat. The only occasion when he felt remorse over his evil acts was when Ashwatthama showed him the severed heads of the Pandavas' children.

Thus far, it is evident that Duryodhana was firmly controlled by his emotions, and thereby orchestrated his own destiny. He had a strong resolve and was fearless, obstinate and tenacious. Undoubtedly, he was a great warrior. But his lust for power and hatred of the Pandavas made him totally blind to the concept of dharma. So, steeped in ego, he rejected the wise counsel of elders like Bhishma, Vidura and Drona. He comfortably dismissed all sane counsel and clung to his path of adharma. This shows his personality to have narcissistic, Machiavellian and psychopathic traits along with a hint of sadism where he remorselessly enjoys the injustice and torture he meted out to the Pandavas.

The instances[19] mentioned above from the Mahabharata clearly indicate that Duryodhana inherited several personality traits from his ancestors. However, the conclusions in the book cannot be drawn till we analyse the personality traits of Duryodhana's counterparts—the Pandavas.

IV

PANDAVAS

Positive Counterparts

1

PANDU

A Brief and Uninfluential Life

Pandu was the son of Veda Vyasa and Ambalika, born through the system of niyoga. His life was somehow always shrouded in doubt and mystery. As a young prince, after spending thirty nights with his new wife and with an earlier wife, he left them and went on a world conquest. Ruthlessly reducing 'his rival kings to ashes', in the words of the Mahabharata, he was at the height of glory. Why would that young prince, the long-awaited occupant of the Kuru throne who was adored by all, leave everything behind and go to the forest with his two wives to make hunting his full-time occupation? The Mahabharata tells us that his wives advised him to do so. Why would two young wives of a lustrous young king ask him to leave behind his kingdom and all its comforts, as well as the challenge and responsibility of ruling it, and go and live in the forest to spend his time hunting? The answer to these questions can be understood only after looking at his life in its entirety.

Pandu asked his wives to beget children for him with the help of other men, which was carried out through niyoga.

Why exactly did he have to do that? Was it because of the curse by sage Kindama, whom he saw copulating with his wife in the form of deer and shot dead? Or had Pandu been impotent all along?

The answer to this question can be found by examining a verse in the epic. As Pandu lay dead after engaging in sexual intercourse with his younger wife Madri, Kunti came rushing to the scene. She blamed Madri for their husband's death and said: 'Blessed are you, Madri, and more fortunate than I am. For, you were able to see the face of the king in raptures.' (Dhanya tvam asi bahleeki matto bhagyatara tatha, drshtavatyasi yad vaktram prahrshtasya maheepateh—Adi 124.21).[1] Kunti was referring to the ecstasy of a sexual climax that still lingered on dead Pandu's face. Kunti had perhaps seen this expression on the faces of the four different men who had fathered her children, but never on the face of her husband Pandu.

The Mahabharata minutely tell us that a smile lingered on Pandu's face, even in his death. And yet nothing in the Mahabharata tells us that Pandu had rejected Kunti sexually. From all we know, he was deeply in love with her from the day she chose him for a husband to the last day of his life.

This explains a lot of things. For instance, it explains why Bhishma was in a hurry to get him a second wife. The Mahabharata does not tell us how long it was before Bhishma went and got Madri as a second wife for Pandu. It could have been immediately after his marriage to Kunti or after sometime had passed. Getting young Pandu a second wife as soon as he was married does not make sense, unless it was meant to be an urgent political alliance. Though, that does not seem to be the case. Besides, Bhishma would have been very reluctant to offer his nephew two young beautiful wives at the same time, considering the disastrous past of Pandu's father Vichitravirya.

The second marriage should have been after some time with an important reason behind it. It was not a love marriage, but an arranged one. A political alliance does not seem to have been a desperate necessity, which leaves us with another strong possibility. The first marriage had failed to produce what the Kuru-Bharata family needed desperately: Pandu's heir, in case anything happened to the young king. He had failed to produce an offspring with his first wife so far. Bhishma, who had no idea that Kunti was already a mother before her marriage, must have assumed that the fault lay with her (the woman was the first suspect in such cases, and getting a second wife was the easiest solution for the man, particularly a king). He might not even have considered the possibility that Pandu was impotent. And Pandu might not have revealed it himself, nor did Kunti. So Bhishma got Pandu a second wife, Madri.

It also explains why Pandu left on a world conquest exactly thirty nights after his wedding with Madri. That must have been a terrible month for the impotent Pandu. He now had two wives, each as beautiful as a goddess, and yet there was nothing he could do to improve his sexual life. So, a bitter, frustrated and furious Pandu gathered his army and left on a world conquest. He had failed to prove his potency. But he could prove himself in the battlefield. Pandu was savage in the battlefield, as the Mahabharata tells us. He did not just win battles, but burnt his rivals to ashes. He then came back victorious, bringing enormous wealth with him.

The Mahabharata uses a very unusual expression to describe the triumphant Pandu on his return to Hastinapur: 'punar-mudita-vahanah'. This means that on the return journey to Hastinapur, even 'his vehicles were happy, once again'. That is to say that Pandu was happy once again. And even his vehicles, his horses and elephants, reflected his happiness. The words 'once again' are significant because they imply that it was not a happy Pandu that had left on the conquest, but an unhappy one.

Also, surprisingly, Pandu did not add the conquered wealth to the treasury of the Kurus, as would have been expected of him. Instead, he distributed it among Bhishma, Satyavati, Ambika, Ambalika, Vidura, his friends, etc. It is as though he wanted them all to see the amount of wealth and glory he had attained, to certify how much of a man he was. There was so much wealth, that it is said that Dhritarashtra later performed a hundred ashwamedha sacrifices with it. This shows that Pandu possibly possessed narcissistic traits.[2] His need for excessive attention and admiration can only be considered dysfunctional, resulting in exploitative acts or behaviours.

After this, he did an extremely strange thing. The long-awaited ruler of Hastinapur, Pandu had just taken over the reins of the kingdom. He had to prove himself as a competent king by successfully winning battles. But immediately after the battles, on his wives' urging he decided to leave Hastinapur. He went to the jungle with them and engaged in hunting. Why would Pandu do something like that? A strong possibility that comes to mind is that he did not want Bhishma to bring him yet another wife. He had no answers to his accusing glances, along with those of his mother and grandmother. He must have discussed this with his wives, from whom he could not have hidden the facts of the matter. With their wisdom and understanding, they must have advised him to leave everything and go to the jungle with them. No one would torment him there.

If Pandu had been impotent all along, then it was not the curse of the sage that had forced him to have his children begotten by other men. What Pandu actually did to the deer couple may have been a later addition to the story. What might have happened is that Pandu saw a male and a female deer copulating in the jungle and shot them dead. That's all.

But then why would, as we asked earlier, a cultured man who was a scion of the noble Bharata dynasty do such a thing? Perhaps, for the same reasons that caused his impotence. There is every reason to believe that Pandu's impotence was psychological. Pandu was physically fit. He was a mighty warrior, a terror to his enemies. Except for the paleness of his skin, there was no mention of any physical deficiency in him. And he died while engaged in a sexual act with his wife. All these point to his impotence as having been psychological and not physical.

Literature on the psychopathology of impotence tells us that psychopathological impotence may be associated with a very restrictive upbringing concerning sex, negative attitudes toward sex and negative or traumatic sexual experiences. Other deep-seated causal factors include unconscious feelings of hostility, fear, inadequacy or guilt. All of these are symptoms of neuroticism. The study also states that men with sexual dysfunction present significantly higher levels of neuroticism when compared to sexually healthy men. Moreover, regression analysis indicates neuroticism as the best predictor of sexual functioning. Regarding psychopathology, men with sexual problems presented significantly higher levels of depressive symptoms. Therefore, the study concluded that personality dimensions and psychopathology play an important role in male sexual functioning. The results may have important clinical implications.[3]

Let us look at how Pandu was conceived. The niyoga was not a happy incident for Pandu's mother Ambalika or for her sister Ambika, who was Dhritarashtra's mother. Ambalika knew it would be Vyasa performing the niyoga. Yet when the sage entered her room and approached her bed, she was horrified and turned pale. The act of conceiving Pandu was one of indescribable horror and repugnance to his mother. The horror the sisters felt was so great that they refused to undergo the torture a second time and sent a maid in their place when they were forced to. After the conception and birth of Pandu and Dhritarashtra, both sisters withdrew into shells that they never emerged from.[4] The palace of Hastinapur was packed with maids and slaves. It was impossible that a fatherless child with a negligent mother did not hear palace rumours about his birth. It should not surprise us if he heard what happened in graphic details. How a young sensitive mind would react to such talk is impossible to predict. And Pandu was definitely a very sensitive child and grew up to be a very sensitive man. In Pandu's case, it apparently resulted in an unconscious horror of sex, for what he heard concerned his own mother. The images that the gossip generated could have played repeatedly in his mind, eventually rendering him psychologically impotent. It is not impossible to imagine that every time he approached one of his wives, the image of his mother and the horrible experience she had been subjected to flashed in front of his eyes.

From the picture presented of him in the Mahabharata, Pandu appears to have been a man capable of great love. At least to begin with. As a child he must have loved his mother deeply, as was shown by his act of offering part of the wealth he had brought from the conquest at her feet. Listening to all the palace gossip as a child must have confused him. It could have led him, like countless other children, to think that sex was something horrid that men did to women. It wouldn't be surprising if he felt that he too, was somehow responsible, in subjecting his mother to that horrid act. Partly because he was a man and partook in the crime that some men afflict at women, and partly because his mother had to undergo it for the sake of his birth. The result could have been a very powerful sense of guilt.

Another angle that must be looked into is Bhishma's effect on the child and adolescent Pandu, with regard to his sexual development. The Mahabharata tells us that it was mostly Bhishma who brought him up. Here was a man who had become a legend in his own lifetime, partly because he had denied himself of sex. Pandu seems to have had his share of all the elements that cause psychopathological impotence.

In the spiritual interpretation of the Mahabharata, Vyasa's four sons were the embodiments of the four purusharthas—the goals of human life. Shuka was the embodiment of the paramapurushartha of moksha, liberation. Vidura of dharma, righteousness. Dhritarashtra of artha, wealth and possessiveness. And Pandu was the embodiment of kama, desire. He was lust embodied. Therefore, it is easy to imagine that Pandu's sons may have inherited these behavioural dispositions. An example I explain later is how, on reading the vigorously passionate expressions of the Pandavas when they first saw Draupadi, Kunti decided to marry her to all five brothers.

2

KUNTI

An Inconsistent DNA to Pandavas

Pandu was married to Kunti, the adopted daughter of King Kuntibhoja. Her real father was King Sura of the Yadava clan. Kuntibhoja had adopted her and used her to serve a Brahmin visiting his court. This Brahmin was known both for his irascibility and his great magical powers. Kunti served him so well that he blessed the king and gave Kunti several mantras with which she could summon any god to father her child. In her childish curiosity, Kunti, while still unmarried, used one mantra and called upon Surya. He appeared immediately and begot a son on her. Frightened, Kunti put the child in a box, with some gold and jewellery, and set it afloat in the river. The boy was found and adopted by the suta Adhiratha, and came to be known as Karna.

Kunti was the matriarch of the Pandava household, possessing verbal strength and decisive articulation. Matrilineality predominated in the birth of the Pandavas (through the convention of niyoga) and an example of it can be observed in Bhima's revelation of his identity to his brother Hanuman. He said 'I am a Kshatriya hero, a descendent of Kuru race and a son of Kunti' (Rajagopalachari, 2009, p. 159).[1] This statement aligned him to matrilineal preponderance. Kunti's authority was also highlighted during her instructive stipulation of dharma to her sons while they lived in the forest, and her model of good kingship in Udyog Parva cannot be ignored. Her decisiveness in abandoning Karna and concealing it till the end was aligned with her primary concern—the 'welfare of the dynastic line of Pandu' (Chaitanya 1985, pp. 152–59).[2] Moreover, it was her intelligence that allowed her to summon Dharma first. This assured that her actions were accompanied by legitimization of levirate.

She played a pivotal role in sanctifying the marriage of Draupadi to all five Pandavas. She 'with her motherly instincts read her sons' desire to go to Panchala and win Draupadi' (Rajagopalachari, 2009, p. 68).[3] This decision of hers was not inadvertent, but a planned strategy as it solved a dual purpose—to align the Pandavas with a common wife (symbol of unity), and to be supported by strong allies. In other words, Draupadi acted as Kunti's deputy, who during their exile in the forest performed the motherly functions, one of which was to win back the throne of Hastinapur.

Also, Kunti was the one who ensured Krishna's allegiance to the Pandavas, which inspired a righteous victory. Just for the welfare of her sons, she swallowed her pride, approached Karna and appealed to him to join the Pandavas, even though he refused. To him, she said 'Son, all the Kauravas will be destroyed in the battle. Let it be as you say. Who can fight fate' (Karve 1994, pp. 67–86).[4] Not just a selfish instigation, it can be interpreted as her desire to protect Karna from a certain providence. Though she couldn't sway him, she made him promise not to slay any of her sons except Arjuna. This was another intelligent move by Kunti.

Due to Pandu's impotence, he wanted Kunti to have sons from another man. But she told him about the mantras that Durvasa had given her. With Pandu's consent she summoned three gods to father his sons. Dharma, or Yudhishthira, was born of Yama, also called Dharma or the god of death and regulation. A year later, her second son Bhima was born of Vayu, the Wind God. He was a giant in stature and power. The next year, her third son Arjuna was born of Indra, the king of gods. These three sons are called Kaunteya (sons of Kunti) in the Mahabharata. Pandu's other wife Madri begged him to ask Kunti to give her a mantra too, and Kunti acquiesced. Madri called the twin gods Ashvini and gave birth to twins Nakula and Sahadeva. They were called Madreya, sons of Madri. All five children were collectively known as the Pandavas, the sons of Pandu.

After Pandu and Madri's death, Kunti returned to Hastinapur, along with the five infants, the half-charred bodies of Pandu and Madri, and many Brahmins. Pandu and Madri were cremated again with ceremonial rites. Kunti lived on at the Hastinapur court, and her five sons, together with the sons of Gandhari, were brought up under the tutelage of Bhishma. A keen rivalry soon developed between these five and their cousins.

Kunti seems to have been born to endure only sorrow. A dozen years of happiness were too few to compensate her for her long life of sorrow and humiliations. Every man in her life contributed to her unhappiness. She never said anything directly to blame her husband but she did reproach her father bitterly. 'As a spendthrift squanders his money unthinking, so did my father give me away when yet a girl to his friend.'[5] Though one feels pity for her, in her own estimate, her condition, though sometimes sorrowful, was never lowly or pitiable. She did not think that riches or material comforts were necessary for the happiness of a Kshatriya woman.

Her biological father gave her away to a friend. One lifelong sorrow was borne of this action. Her adoptive father gave her in marriage to an impotent man; and the rest of her sorrows were a result of this union.

Pandu, her husband was the king of Hastinapur. Kunti, therefore, was the queen. Pandu, as he became the king, went on a conquering expedition, defeated many kings and brought immense wealth as tribute. He presented it all to his blind elder brother Dhritarashtra, and himself went to live in the Himalayan forests with his two wives, Kunti and Madri. All the Kuru kings were addicted to hunting but that could not have been his reason, for they did not take their queens along with them to the hunts. Pandu had gone to the forest with the intention of living there. Did he intend that some other man would beget children on his wives? Did he wish to carry out this plan away from the capital so that nobody found out the identity of the fathers of the children? However, at the end, Kunti returned with five children.

Pandu begged Kunti to conceive sons from some Brahmin. It was at this point that Kunti told him about the boon given to her by Durvasa. This was also an opportunity for her to reveal the existence of Karna. According to the custom of the time, when niyoga was an acceptable practice, such a child could have become a legitimate son of Pandu. However, Kunti at that time had no idea what had happened to Karna, whether he had lived or not. Therefore, she never said anything about this child.

Madri burnt herself on Pandu's funeral pyre, but the life which Kunti was left to drudge alone was equally hard, if not harder. Kunti comes across as a tough and just woman on this occasion. In a patriarchal, polygynous society, a woman's status depended entirely on the position of a man—either her father or husband or son. The highest stature that a Kshatriya woman could aspire to was to be the eldest wife of a crowned king and to give birth to his eldest son. To have more sons than the other wives was also a means of securing, if not the love of a husband, then at least the position of the chief queen. Kunti did not want the stigma of being barren to be attached to Madri, but she was certainly not going to allow the junior and more beautiful queen to have more children than herself. She knew that Pandu's preference for the beautiful Madri was due to spite and jealousy. Since the security of Kunti's sons depended on the king's life, as in due course her sons would succeed their father to the throne, Kunti was highly protective of Pandu's life.

Pandu was the fourth man in her life to contribute to her miseries: her two fathers, the illegitimate son and now her husband. When everything had seemed within reach, his one rash act dashed Kunti's hopes. Pandu and Madri escaped to death, but Kunti had to traverse the hard, stony path of her life alone.

During the period when they were hiding in the forest, after the burning of Laakshyagriha, it was she who encouraged Bhima to become the lover of and to marry a rakshasa (demon) woman—Hidimbaa. This woman was very useful to the Pandavas, and later, her son gave his life for them in the war. Kunti got Bhima to kill the demon Baka. And it was she, as mentioned earlier, who determined that Draupadi was to be the wife of all her five sons. With this move, Madri's and Kunti's sons were welded into one unbreakable whole. Later, this proved to be an effective bar against all of Duryodhana's plans to set them against one another. Kunti had always given, not only her impartial care but also her heart to Madri's sons. Towards her own sons she was stern and dutiful, while there was a bond of genuine affection between her and Madri's sons.

Kunti's suffering and hope during the years of her sons' exile is very well described in Udyoga Parva.[6] Draupadi chose to go into exile with her husbands, leaving her children behind. Kunti, though not in exile, suffered greater agonies because she had to live among enemies and witness their prowess and prosperity. When Krishna went to negotiate a treaty with the Kauravas, he called on her. When he left Hastinapur after the negotiations had fallen through, she sent messages with him for all her sons.

She reminded Bhima and Arjuna not to forget their humiliation. Her main appeal, however, was to Dharma. This was her eldest son, the heir to the throne. But he desired neither war nor conquest. She said:

> Yudhishthira is the very soul of dharma. Tell him, 'By your behavior you are destroying dharma. You are aware only of one dharma, the dharma of the sluggish unlearned Brahmins who are caught in a mesh' of words. But Brahmadeva created the Kshatriyas from his powerful chest so that they live by the force of their arms and protect their subjects. A king who forgets his dharma goes to hell and drags with him all his subjects. What was yours by the right of inheritance from your father has been lost. Recover it. Make it your own. Your behavior pleases the enemy. No shame is greater than that I should live on other people's charity while you are still alive. Remember the dharma of the Kshatriyas. Do not throw your ancestors, younger brothers and yourself into hell.

Her words clearly reveal her mortifications, her hopes for the future and her unbending will. These words motivated the Pandavas to agree to wage war on the Kauravas to get their share of inheritance. Kunti was the unifying force behind the Pandavas, guarding them and keeping them safe at all times. It was her strong will and unending endurance that helped her sons achieve what they did at the end of the war. If not for her, Yudhishthira would never have agreed to go to war with the Kauravas, and it was because of his initiative that the other Pandavas followed suit. Kunti was the reason why the Pandava household was a tight-knit family. Had she not deliberately asked the Pandavas to share Draupadi among themselves as a common wife, they would not have stayed united till the end. Her only mistake was her curiosity which bore her Karna, and then abandoning him. But this one incident is not sufficient to tag her personality traits as negative. For the most part, her flaws can be pinned as minor human flaws that any normal human being could possess as a result of his or her circumstances.

Apparently, Kunti's actions and behaviours are inconsistent to those of the other Kurus. She displays extraordinary courage and emotional stability throughout the epic. The aforementioned instances in the Mahabharata clearly indicate that she was a pillar of support to Pandu and his five sons. She was certainly a DNA disruptor, from whom the Pandavas inherited courage, emotional stamina, family orientation, and finally a commitment to dharma as life's guiding principle. These traits were likely missing in the Kuru lineage before she came along.

3

PANDAVAS

Evil Actions and Connivances

While reading the Mahabharata, one gets familiar with the endless number of characters, and finds that each character is propelled by an alternate reason, which shapes his/her fate. The striking likeness of these characters to people around us, in our present-day society, is the thing that makes the Mahabharata a most fascinating book.

In this chapter, I will be focusing on those deeds of the Pandavas that cannot be regarded as entirely ethical according to the classical definition of dharma. Since, from the beginning to the end, it has always been pointed out by various characters in the epic that the Pandavas were on the side of 'dharma' and the Kauravas symbolized 'adharma', we will see that on many occasions, the Pandavas too resorted to means and methods that were not ethical or moral in the truest sense. The Pandavas too were the culprits of some vicious misdeeds—largely some tricks committed in the battle upon Krishna's urgings. In the eyes of the epic's Vaishnava editors, who glorify Lord Krishna and try to establish a pro-Pandava moral valence even in the

107

face of immoral actions on both sides, all of Duryodhana's wrongdoings are contained within a single flaw: his blindness to Krishna's divinity. The rules and structures that signify 'dharma' get substantially diluted on the battlefield. Krishna resorts to several strategies that can be justified only if one submits to the idea of the Kauravas representing 'adharma' who are to be vanquished at any cost, and even then, by subscribing to the principle that means justify ends. The lie uttered by Yudhishthira to deceive Drona, Bhima's striking Duryodhana below his waist, and Arjuna's killing of Karna when he was unarmed, are some of these questionable strategic measures.

When we examine the Pandavas' actions individually as well as collectively, we can see that at times they too resorted to adharma—unfair means to achieve their ends. Yudhishthira hangs on so emphatically to nonviolence and peace that it turns into the very purpose behind the horrendous Kurukshetra war. The inherent quality in Yudhishthira to maintain a strategic distance from any conflict is demonstrated on numerous occasions, as he doesn't strike back at any of Duryodhana's insults, settles down with half the kingdom with no grievance, accepts defeat in the game of dice and the resulting exile for thirteen years. Even after all the dishonorable treatment meted out to him, his wife and his siblings, he is anxious to avoid war by negotiating for five pitiful villages in place of the whole kingdom of Hastinapur. His brothers, being the obedient younger ones, agree to all his decisions.

Though Yudhishthira is always associated with an exemplary sense of 'dharma', one does find in him the misgivings and uncertainties that plague an ordinary person. His weakness for peace and nonviolence, and his reservations about his stature in Hastinapur are at the forefront. But before we delve deeper, it is important to understand what one means by 'dharma' as it is always rendered synonymous with Yudhishthira, the 'Dharmaputra' (son of Yama, the lord of dharma). Dharma, if translated into English, can be referred to as laws that every individual abides by, and which empower him with the strength and the courage to face any moral, ethical challenges in life.[1]

The Actions

The first instance where one gets a glimpse of Yudhishthira's weaker side is when the Pandavas are in disguise in Ekachakrapura, after they escape an attempt on their lives in the palace of lac. They seek refuge in a Brahmin's house, who provides them with shelter and food. One day, Kunti finds the Brahmin and his family in extreme grief and asks them the cause of their distress. The Brahmin tells her that the villagers of Ekachakrapura are tormented by a rakshasa named Baka. He would enter the village at his convenience and devour the villagers and their cattle. So, the villagers made a pact with him that each day one member from a family would bring the rakshasa food and drink. The rakshasa agreed to it, but he would also devour the person who brought him the food. It happened to be the Brahmin's family's turn to send one of their members to the rakshasa the following day. Thus, they were grief-stricken, trying to decide who would be the one to go. Upon hearing the pitiful story and deciding to help the Brahmin and the villagers, Kunti volunteers to send her son Bhima, whose physical strength and prowess was matchless. Moreover, she feels indebted to the Brahmin who had provided them with shelter when they were in dire need of it. She convinces the Brahmin to accept the help, and ordains Bhima to take the Brahmin's place in taking the food to the rakshasa. Bhima accepts the offer willingly and goes to meet the rakshasa. When Yudhishthira learns of this, one is surprised to find him angry and upset at his mother's actions. He admonishes her for her rash decision, as she had placed Bhima in a perilous situation. Though one expects him to be worried for his brother, here he is more worried about losing Bhima's support and strength in fighting the Kauravas. He bursts forth, saying:

> What rash act hast thou done, O mother! . . . That Bhima, relying on whose arms we sleep happily in the night and hope to recover the kingdom of which we have been deprived by the covetous son of Dhritarashtra, that hero of immeasurable energy, remembering whose prowess Duryodhana and Shakuni do not sleep a wink during the whole night and by whose prowess we were rescued from the palace of lac and various other dangers, that Bhima who caused the death of Purochana, and relying on whose might we regard ourselves as having already slain the sons of Dhritarashtra and acquired the whole earth with all her wealth, upon what considerations, O mother, hast thou resolved upon abandoning him?'[2]

A person who was hitherto hailed as calm, unperturbed and wise, suddenly reveals the ugly side of his fear and unease about his future, thereby exhibiting neurotic characteristics. One wonders where his sense of justice and dharma went when he questions his mother for helping a family that had given them refuge when they most needed it.

At this juncture one wonders if he is any different from people like Duryodhana, Dhritarashtra, Shakuni and the rest. But the slip is only momentary as he quickly gathers his wits upon Kunti's wise counsel. As she points out Bhima's invincible strength, which is impossible to beat, and also to the dharma of protecting the weak and the needy, he calms down instantly, his faith restored in his mother's wisdom and

Bhima's prowess. One sees in him the willingness to accept his mistake and correct himself, but there is also a nagging thought if the reconciliation is too quick to be natural. Does he actually accept his mistake or does he accept his mother's decision because he finds no other recourse? It might seem like overanalyzing a natural reaction of fear and shock when one's younger brother has been sent to face a rakshasa of immense power, but when this incident is juxtaposed with other similar incidents where Yudhishthira manipulates things to gain the utmost benefit, one does see that he had in him the shrewdness to turn things around in his favour. Draupadi's swayamvara and her marriage to the five Pandavas is one such incident.

As we discuss the shortcomings of Yudhishthira, we should also keep in mind that these were not predominant, unitary traits in him, but temporary lapses that any mortal being is capable of. He is quick to accept his mistakes and recover from censure to mould himself into a better person.

When Arjuna wins Draupadi's hand in the guise of a Brahmin youth, the assembled kings deem it a great insult and challenge Drupada (Draupadi's father) to fight them. As Arjuna stands in support of Drupada, Bhima joins Arjuna. In all this confusion, Yudhishthira, with Nakula and Sahadeva, quietly leaves the place unnoticed. It is obvious that he reaches home before Arjuna and Bhima return with the bride. One can view this act of Yudhishthira cynically, a perspective usually not used for him. What follows is an excellent example of his astuteness in perceiving and analyzing the pros and cons of a particular incident, and taking appropriate decisions. He manipulates, and possibly orchestrates, an excellent drama, as Kunti unwittingly asks the brothers to equally divide amongst themselves whatever they had earned. It is possible that Yudhishthira who had left Drupada's court much earlier had informed his mother on the outcome of the swayamvara. Moreover, Kunti cannot be so forgetful as to ask her sons to share their alms, as they had left for the swayamvara with her blessings. Hence, it does not take much time to deduce that Yudhishthira had seen to it that Draupadi became the common wife of all five brothers. He puts his mother in front of him, as he knows that his mother's words will not be denied, and also that he cannot initiate this act. He was capable of playing behind the scenes. Here, Draupadi's consent to be the wife of all the Pandavas was completely ignored (even though she, who unhesitatingly refused to marry a suta putra in her swayamvara, and was capable of fiercely defending her stance in front of everyone, did not really show her unwillingness in this situation either.) Since, all the Pandavas did not object to Yudhishthira, (even though Arjuna might have had discontent in his mind but agreed to stay united under Yudhishthira's supervision), it could be seen as a collective decision from their side. Moreover, the fact that the other Pandavas desired her, despite Draupadi having been won by their brother Arjuna, was enough to determine that their decision to marry Draupadi was also laced with lust. Even though, according to traditional Indian values, the elder brother's wife is considered equivalent to one's mother, and the younger brother's wife is considered equivalent to a sister.

Though on surface it might seem manipulative, but when the larger picture of the Pandavas' unity emerges, it is easy to see Yudhishthira's political shrewdness, which was desired in a Kshatriya at that time. Of course, the argument arises whether it is appropriate to ignore Draupadi's interests, while ensuring better prospects for the Pandavas. But one also has to keep in mind the precarious situation of the Pandavas whose lives were under constant threat from the Kauravas. At any cost, they had to gather support and the power to shield themselves from Duryodhana; and Drupada would be a powerful ally. Further, they had to remain united to take on the Kauravas. Yudhishthira had to ensure that there wouldn't be any discord among the Pandavas regarding Draupadi—as he sees the eagerness in all their eyes when looking at Draupadi.[3] Thus, Yudhishthira instantly declares that Draupadi will be their common wife. Not only did Yudhishthira predict dissention among the brothers on Draupadi's pretext, he also realized the complications that would arise if Draupadi wedded only Arjuna. What if Drupada extended his support to Arjuna alone? What would be the position of the other brothers in that case? As Yudhishthira did not want even a remote chance of Arjuna deserting his brothers, he took a firm step in eliminating the problem even before it arose. Thus, Yudhishthira's decision to make Draupadi the common wife of all five brothers can be seen as an excellent example of his highly evolved emotional skills. The Pandavas' wedding to Draupadi had more than political implications and emotional complications. These actions by Yudhishthira clearly indicate that he was not a simple novice or as 'dharmic' as portrayed in the epic. There is a possibility of secondary versions, perspectives and viewpoints.

When Duryodhana's character was analysed, it was seen how cunningly he tricked Shalya (Nakula and Sahadeva's maternal uncle) to support him in the war. Yudhishthira goes a step ahead and approaches Shalya at a time when he is guilty of extending his support to Duryodhana. This again, could be seen as a collective decision of the Pandavas, since the brothers followed Yudhishthira in administrative decisions without questioning his authority. Taking full advantage of Shalya's guilt, he makes Shalya promise, that at a crucial juncture when Shalya was Karna's charioteer, he would demoralize Karna by insulting him and praising Arjuna. He requests Shalya, 'There is no doubt that thou wilt act as the charioteer of Karna. Thou must damp the spirits of Karna then by recounting the praises of Arjuna.'[4] This incident gains significance when one comprehends the master craftsman in Yudhishthira. He is shrewd enough to know that in the crucial battle between Arjuna and Karna, Shalya would be chosen as Karna's charioteer, as his skills are unmatched by anyone but Lord Krishna. Next, he knows how important it was for Karna to prove himself better than Arjuna. Karna was plagued by the insecurity of not knowing his biological parents. His entire life was a torment as he unsuccessfully fights for recognition equivalent to that of Arjuna. Not only is he denied this recognition, but is jeered at and insulted as a person of doubtful parentage, in spite of his extraordinary military skills. Yudhishthira chooses to strike at Karna's vulnerability to demoralize him, and thus ensure victory for the Pandavas. Right from the day Karna steps into the arena, challenging Arjuna to fight with him, Yudhishthira identifies a formidable foe in him. Karna's military skills terrified Yudhishthira as he '. . . was impressed with the belief that there was no warrior on earth like unto Karna.'[5] This knowledge makes Yudhishthira not just cautious of war, but he also starts strengthening the Pandavas in the eventuality of war. In spite of knowing that Karna was an unparalleled warrior and the only one capable of defeating Arjuna, he asked Shalya to humiliate him and call him incompetent in the battlefield. Even though there is nothing dishonest in this act, it can still be regarded as misconduct for a person like Yudhishthira who claimed to speak nothing but the truth.

There is no justification for Yudhishthira's behaviour in this case. The condition put forth to Shalya by Yudhishthira, on behalf of all the Pandavas, was only based on fear and insecurity, because they knew that Karna was powerful and skilled enough to take Arjuna down in battle. The reason could have been battleground strategy and not an unethical practice per se. And since it did not violate the rules of war, it could be said that they were trying to provoke Karna's insecurity, leading him to make a bad move, which they could use to their advantage.

In the Laakshyagriha burning incident, six Nishadas (one Nishada woman and five of her children) were poisoned and killed as decoy to fake the death of Kunti and the five Pandavas—an act not much talked about.

The only justification of this abhorrent act could be that they were trying to survive in a world where gross injustice had been done to them as well. But it is not a good enough excuse to kill six innocent people. (I believe they could have fooled the Kauravas by using other means to depict their death in the accident.)

Yudhishthira practiced nonviolence, even in extreme situations that led the Pandavas to unpredictable miseries. For instance, consider the episode of Draupadi's modesty outraged by Jayadratha, Duryodhana's sister Dusshala's husband. Mesmerized by Draupadi's beauty, Jayadratha forces her on to his chariot and carries her away. As the Pandavas come to know about this, they hunt him down and rescue Draupadi. Unable to stand against the five invincible warriors, Jayadratha flees. Arjuna and Bhima set out to find him. The enraged Draupadi demands Jayadratha's life. But Yudhishthira very calmly instructs his brothers, 'O thou of mighty arms, remembering (our sister) Dusshala and the celebrated Gandhari, thou shouldst not slay the king of Sindhu even though he is wicked!'[6] Exercising nonviolence against a person who has violated his wife's modesty beats all logic. One wonders how could a person who is compassionate towards the antagonist's sister fail to understand his wife's grievance. Misplaced compassion has its own serious repercussions. The defeated and insulted Jayadratha seeks divine blessings to defeat the Pandavas. Lord Shiva grants him the boon that, save Arjuna, he will be able to defeat the other four brothers in battle. At Kurukshetra, when Arjuna is elsewhere fighting the Samsaptakas, Jayadratha defeats Yudhishthira, Bhima, Nakula and Sahadeva and is instrumental in killing Arjuna's young son Abhimanyu.

Yudhishthira's inaction remains a characteristic trait in him throughout his life. He stays an indecisive person plagued by self-doubt. Lacking initiative, he does not have the confidence to go ahead with the rajasuya yajna—a ritual to claim the kingship. It does not suffice that his official priest Dhaumya, the divine sage Narada, and his illustrious brothers try to convince him. He seeks Krishna's advice too, before hesitatingly accepting to perform the rajasuya yajna. Still, he is uncomfortable with Jarasandha's prowess, and is not sure if Bhima and Arjuna can conquer him. It is with such fits and starts that he undertook any venture. Aware of his trait, Kunti sends him a firm message through Krishna before the Kurukshetra war. Scared that Yudhishthira might back out of the war and concede his rightful kingdom to the Kauravas, she narrates the conversation between princess Vidula and her son. Vidula's son was of a similar disposition; lacking the initiative and motivation to win back the kingdom he had lost. Vidula's fiery words of inspiration enabled her son to break free from his stupor and gather the drive to defeat his enemies. The message is loud and clear—Yudhishthira too should remind himself of his foremost duties as a Kshatriya and take up arms against injustice. Like Dhritarashtra, who is caught between a sense of justice and his love for Duryodhana, Yudhishthira too is constantly caught between the desire to lead a peaceful life in pursuit of spiritual knowledge, and his duty as a Kshatriya to take up arms against his enemies and protect his subjects. This often leaves him in unenviable situations where he earns the displeasure of his brothers and wife.

I don't see any justification for this behaviour by Yudhishthira and his obedient brothers. Being a Kshatriya, they should have fought with Jayadratha, who outraged their wife's dignity. His compassion seems misplaced, wherein he sympathized with Dusshala and Gandhari but not Draupadi.

If we look at other minor instances where the Pandavas acted in an unfair manner, then their childhood cannot be ignored. In their defence, it can be said that they were not mature enough to understand the consequences of their acts. But then, a young Duryodhana too should not be held responsible for his evil scheme to poison Bhima in their childhood. Kohli describes that when the Pandavas and the Kauravas were children, Bhima, with his immense physical strength, was a bully and would torture the younger Kauravas, sometimes almost killing them in the process. As Yudhishthira was older than Bhima and the Kauravas, it was his duty to restrain Bhima from torturing his younger cousins. However, he did nothing of this sort, and we can conclude he turned a blind eye towards Bhima's misdeeds.

Bhima being a bully in his childhood could be true, however, his intentions were never ill, and he meant no permanent harm to the Kauravas. Unlike him, Bhima did not have any evil intentions to kill Duryodhana and his brothers to inherit the kingdom. His bullying was only a show of his physical strength that he never failed to boast about. And since it wasn't unethical per se, Yudhishthira never said anything about it unless it crossed the limit of dignified behaviour on his part. For example, once Bhima compared Karna to a dog due to his low-caste affiliation.

However, it must be kept in mind that the caste system (or the varna system) was one of the fundamental tenets of the society at that time. Violating it was considered to be unethical. Therefore, involving lower-caste people in an upper-class ritual was forbidden. Each of the varnas took their roles in the society seriously, and any digression from it was taboo.

Another instance that points out the misdeeds of Bhima (supported by all the Pandavas), was during their first self-designed exile, when he met Hidimbaa, and despite no fault of hers, was about to kill her. (Though later she was spared due to Yudhishthira's politically motivated intervention.) The story began after the Pandavas escaped from the Laakshyagriha and reached a dense forest. Tired and exhausted, they all fell asleep at night, except Bhima, who kept a watch. In the same forest lived Hidimbaa along with her brother Hidimba, who was a very powerful rakshasa. He smelled the Pandavas resting at a distance, and asked Hidimbaa to lure the well-built Bhima so they could prey on him. Hidimbaa confronted Bhima but fell in love with him. She assumed the form of a very beautiful lady, approached Bhima and expressed her desire to marry him. She also revealed her true identity and her brother's intentions. Bhima refused to accept her as his wife and confronted Hidimba. A great fight took place, which resulted in Hidimba getting killed. After killing Hidimba, Bhima wanted to kill Hidimbaa too as he thought that she might want to avenge her brother's death. Yudhishthira stopped Bhima from committing such a deed. Hidimbaa then begged Kunti to allow Bhima to marry her, as she was deeply in love with him, and also because she was all alone now. Kunti ordered Bhima to marry Hidimbaa. Bhima, on Yudhishthira's counsel, agreed on the condition that he could leave her once she bore a child with him. Hidimbaa agreed and they got married. Within a year, Hidimbaa gave birth to a son. They named him Ghatotkacha. Ghatotkacha went on to become a great warrior and an important figure in the Mahabharata war. What should be noted here is the fact that Bhima abandoned his wife once a son was born to them, and never fulfilled the duties of a father to Ghatotkacha. Not only was this act an unfair one, but also immoral. He knew that they could ask his powerful son Ghatotkacha to help him during the war later, and that was the only reason he married Hidimbaa.

Kunti was aware of her and her children's precarious position. She, along with her children, was a fugitive escaping an assassination bid, and was in desperate need of shelter and comfort. Away from the restrictive gaze of the society and living in seclusion, the Pandavas and Kunti had no inhibitions in mixing freely with Hidimbaa and her son. Though they were helped by Hidimbaa, they probably realized that if they stayed there for a longer period, they would be doomed to a life of seclusion, and deprived of their rightful share in their kingdom. Since, they had no permanent place to stay and no reliable shelter, they decided to leave Hidimbaa and move on. It's possible that Kunti and the other Pandavas were feeling apprehensive that Bhima might grow too fond of Hidimbaa, and choose to stay with her permanently. There was also the possibility of a loss of face if a rakshasi girl became the first daughter-in-law of the Pandu family, or even the entire younger generation of the Kuru princes, as Duryodhana was yet to be married at that time.

Coming to Arjuna and his individual acts, we come across the story of Ekalavya. Though Arjuna never makes a deliberate, obvious comment on his wish to become the greatest undisputed archer, he leaves no stone unturned to achieve the same. If not for the episode of Ekalavya that stands as an aberration, Arjuna's success could be admired as the most commendable one. But he proves that in spite of his excellent qualities, he is human enough to give in to baser emotions like jealousy. Drona had promised Arjuna that there would be no archer equivalent to him in the entire universe. But as fate would have it, the Nishada prince Ekalavya comes as an unsuspecting rival to challenge Arjuna's supremacy. It was Ekalavya's cherished dream to become Drona's disciple, and he approached Drona with the same request. But Drona refused him politely saying that he only tutored royal princes, and hence could not accept Ekalavya as his pupil. Undeterred, Ekalavya made a clay image of Drona, instilled him as his guru in his mind, initiated himself as Drona's disciple and started practicing archery. His devotion to his guru made him excel in the skills of archery in no time. Once as the Kaurava and the Pandava princes went into the forests for a hunting expedition, deep into the woods, the hunting dog that accompanied them saw the dark-hued Ekalavya and started barking at him. The Nishada prince playfully shot seven arrows in quick succession to fills the dog's mouth before it could close it. At the same time, the dog was neither injured nor hurt. Stupefied by such deftness of hand, the princes bowed their heads in shame and inquired about the youth. Ekalavya proudly introduced himself as a disciple of guru Drona. Cut to the quick, Arjuna walked up to his guru and asked, 'Thou hadst lovingly told me, clasping me to thy bosom, that no pupil of thine should be equal to me. Why then is there a pupil of thine, the mighty son of the Nishada king, superior to me?'[7] Thereupon, Drona in the name of guru dakshina demanded Ekalavya's thumb which the devoted disciple gave him unhesitatingly. This incident throws light on the depth of Arjuna's desire to remain the undisputed archer of his times, which ignited his jealousy towards Ekalavya. And this desire remained ever burning and undiminished in him till the end. To aim at excelling in one's chosen field cannot be called a weakness, but when the person cannot tolerate someone else with equal or better skills, it leaves much to be desired in his character. While living in Drona's ashrama, Arjuna was unable to beat Ekalavya in archery. Burning with jealousy, Arjuna encouraged or one might say compelled Drona to deprive Ekalavya of his thumb.

In his later years as an adult, one does not find Arjuna giving in to such baser instincts to defeat his rivals. Even his rivalry with Karna is mature and civilized, quite unlike how he felt and acted against Ekalavya. But his pride at being the most skilled and unparalleled archer remained with him. Fortunately for Arjuna, every time he got carried away by his vanity and was about to suffer the consequences, he would quickly regain his senses and focus on solving the problem. The instance of his duel with Lord Shiva, who comes down to Earth to test his skills before blessing him with the divine weapon 'Pasupata' is a good example. Arjuna undertakes severe penance to please Lord Shiva and acquire celestial weapons to help him conquer the Kauravas in the war. Pleased with his austerities, Shiva appears in the form of a 'kirata', a hunter and aims his arrow at the same boar that Arjuna held his aim at. Angry with the kirata for aiming at his chosen target, Arjuna engaged him in a fight. In a few minutes, Arjuna realized that the kirata is invincible, and that he was losing the battle. Hurt and ashamed, he installs Lord Shiva in his mind and starts worshipping him with garlands. He is surprised and shocked to see the very same garlands on the kirata's neck, and realizes that it was none other than Shiva with whom he was fighting. Prostrating before him, he asks for forgiveness, which Lord Shiva readily bestows upon him, and blesses him with the celestial weapons he asks for. If it was pride that forced Arjuna to pick up a fight with the kirata in the first place, then it was the realization of his mistake that drives him to surrender to Lord Shiva. Thus, Arjuna at many instances displays his arrogance in being the best warrior, but is also quick to realize his mistake and take necessary steps to ease the situation. There are no dramatic displays of emotions. Even when he speaks to Drona regarding Ekalavya, it is not aggressively or rudely, but with a gentle strain of disappointment and jealousy, which could not be termed unethical per se.

Another instance that shows the misdeeds of Arjuna was when he broke his vow of Brahmacharya before his twelve years of exile ended. The Pandavas, addressed by Narada, and in consultation with one another, established a rule amongst themselves in the presence of the celestial rishi. They decided that when one of them was spending personal time with Draupadi, if any of the other four saw them, then he must go on an exile into the forests for twelve years, passing his days as a Brahmachari. Because of this understanding, there was no jealousy or dispute between them. However, once a robber stole some cows from the Brahmins in their area. A Brahmin came to Arjuna with his grievance and wanted him to hunt down the robber. Arjuna needed his weapons, which happened to be in the same chamber where Yudhishthira was playing a game of dice with Draupadi at the time and that meant that Arjuna had to violate the privacy clause in order to enter the chamber. He did it regardless, since he considered it his dharma to redress the grievance of his subjects. Though Yudhishthira and Draupadi understood Arjuna's actions and forgave him for it, he was insistent that he should be punished for his actions. Hence, he left on a twelve-year exile. During the exile, he married two other women—Ulupi and Chitrangada. Even though he had vowed to be a Brahmachari during his exile, he broke the vow and married two other women only to leave them soon and move on in his journey. He was similar to Bhima in this respect, since he neglected his fatherly duties towards Iravan and Babruvahana, sons of Ulupi and Chitrangada, respectively.

Though taken aback by Ulupi's direct expression of her sexual desires, at first Arjuna gently refused her advances and explained his condition of having to maintain the vow of Brahmacharya. But Ulupi is perseverant, and goes on to argue that the condition of remaining a Brahmachari applies only in regard to Draupadi and not with any other woman, and thus Arjuna was free to gratify her wishes. His vow would not be broken by accepting Ulupi's advances. Moreover, it was a man's duty to satisfy the woman who openly expressed her love for him. Therefore, even if Arjuna's virtue suffered, it was inconsequential compared to the sin he would have committed by refusing her advances. When Arjuna remained relentless, Ulupi threatened him by saying that she would lay down her life if her wish was unfulfilled. As it was also Arjuna's duty to protect those in misery, he was bound to save her life by granting her wish. Arjuna does not hesitate or procrastinate but spent the night with her. He perceived the desperation in Ulupi's request, and felt that the desperation might catapult into helpless anger, which could drive her to any drastic action that might harm him, and thus he conceded to her wishes. Similarly, he agreed to marry Chitrangada too when she fell in love with him. These decisions weren't rash so as to dishonour him or harm anyone else, but well thought out and balanced. Chitrangada was the princess of Manipur.

There the matriarchal system was followed, which meant that the son born of Chitrangada and Arjuna's union would inherit the throne of Manipur. Therefore, she refused to leave or let her son go with Arjuna and expressed her will to stay in her kingdom.

Arjuna continued on with his exile, travelling to many more places in India, including parts of south India. He then reached Dwaraka, the place where his cousin and close friend Krishna resided. Krishna decided to make his visit comfortable. Arjuna disguised himself as a 'yati' or a nomadic monk. Krishna, however, recognized his true identity and invited him to stay in his palace. Arjuna had heard much about Krishna's beautiful sister, Subhadra, and was eager to meet her. Balarama, in the meantime, had already promised his favourite disciple, Duryodhana, that he would give his sister to him in marriage. Sensing Arjuna's interest as well, Krishna advised him to kidnap Subhadra, before Duryodhana could make her his own. And so, Arjuna kidnapped Subhadra.

The only justification for this act was that, Subhadra, though kidnapped, was also in love with Arjuna and the kidnapping was planned accordingly. At least that is what Lord Krishna told Balarama to pacify his anger since he wanted Subhadra to be married off to Duryodhana.

Arjuna's indecisiveness before and during the war is also worrying. For example, during the war Krishna acted far more as an adviser and counsellor to Arjuna than only as his sarathi. He needed constant push during the war to fight the Kauravas.

The Virata Parva of the epic, which describes the last year of the Pandavas' exile when they lived incognito, is where the subject of dharma is dealt with in depth. The five brothers and Draupadi separated, and entered the service of the king of Virata. When this year of exile drew to a close and

Duryodhana was leaving no stone unturned to expose them so they could be banished again, Keechaka, brother of Sudeshna, the queen of Virata, happened to cast his eye on Draupadi, who as sairandhri was in the queen's employ. She could not ward off his overtures and tried threatening him that her celestial husbands would kill him. These threats were of no avail and the king also turned a blind eye to the misdeeds of his brother-in-law. Yudhishthira and Bhima who witnessed his persecution counselled patience. An irate Draupadi met Bhima alone, and cajoled him to kill Keechaka, which they planned and executed in the dead of night. In the ensuing pandemonium when the ire of Keechaka's half-brothers turned on Draupadi for causing his death, the Pandavas killed over a hundred Upakeechakas. In this way, numerous people were killed by the Pandavas to protect their identity.

I don't find any other justification for this behaviour other than the fact that Yudhishthira wanted to remain calm and not reveal their identity in front of anyone, which could put their lives at stake. Therefore, in order to not be recognized and save their lives, they tried to not react to the insult openly meted out to Draupadi.

As briefly discussed earlier, another collective misdeed of the Pandavas was the burning of the entire Khandava forest, mercilessly massacring innumerable vidhyadhara human tribes, animals and birds who had done no harm to anybody. Not only was this damaging to the ecosystem, but it was also an immoral act that they committed.

This brings us to a very important question. Why do kings exist? To do as they please with their kingdom and their people or to govern the kingdom and ensure the welfare of the land? In traditional Indian philosophy, a king exists only to uphold dharma. And what is dharma?

For God, dharma is ensuring the welfare of all living creatures. For a king, it is the welfare of all his subjects, from the strongest to the weakest. God's kingdom is the whole world; nature, where all animals are given an equal chance to survive. In man's world, the definition of dharma changes. The aim is to provide for the weakest of men. The weakest of men cannot survive in the forest. And so man tames the forest and establishes fields. This cannot be done unless an ecosystem is destroyed. This is brought out in the episode of the burning of Khandavaprastha when Arjuna kills hundreds of plants and animals to set up Indraprastha. Implicit in the idea of human culture and civilization is the destruction of nature, which is not only immoral but also harmful.

However, the burning of the Khandavaprastha, though despicable, was the only option the Pandavas had in order to establish their kingdom. Dhritarashtra and Duryodhana deliberately gave the Pandavas that region of the kingdom, knowing well that they won't be able to live there for long. Taming the entire forest would not have been possible in a short period of time, while they had no other shelter to settle in.

Another misdeed of the Pandavas was when they insulted Duryodhana in their palace of illusions, when he had gone to Indraprastha to attend the rajasuya sacrifice. The palace was full of surprises and illusions because of which Duryodhana slipped and fell into a pool. Draupadi taunted him, 'The blind son of a blind father.' The Pandavas also laughed along and made fun of him. This acted as the last nail in the coffin and enraged by the insult, Duryodhana planned the rigged game of dice that eventually led to the Kurukshetra war.

This was a consequence of a human flaw—to boast and make fun of others—that was also present in the Pandavas, because of which they had to face dire consequences. There was nothing unethical in it, but it certainly showed their character in poor light.

Ultimately, the emphasis on rules and structures of 'dharma' we see in the earlier episodes, gets substantially diluted on the battlefield in Kurukshetra.

The Pandavas, with Krishna's advice, got Indra (who was also Arjuna's father) to trick Karna. Karna was known for his charity and the fact that he always fulfils the wishes of the needy. By disguising as a beggar, Indra got Karna to part with his impenetrable armour and earrings in place of alms. This made Karna vulnerable in war, and ultimately led to his death when he was unarmed and was attacked by Arjuna from behind. At one point during the battle, Karna's chariot wheel got stuck in the mud. He jumped off the chariot to free the wheel, asking Arjuna to pause and consider the most important etiquette of war: never attack one who is unarmed. Upon Krishna's signal, Arjuna went against the rules and used the Anjalika weapon on him, while he was still trying to lift the chariot wheel off the ground. And this is how Karna was slain.

Unable to defeat the great warrior Bhishma, Arjuna, on Krishna's advice, fought standing behind Shikhandi, who was a eunuch and thus, Bhishma could not attack her. Arjuna knew that his grandfather would never attack a woman, and that it was the only way he could ever hope to defeat the mighty doyen. It was on the tenth day of the battle that Bhishma fell to the ground, pierced by Arjuna's multiple arrows. This was all planned by the Pandavas after being advised by Krishna. In this way, in order to meet their ends, they had to take many unethical decisions in the battlefield to defeat the Kauravas and their armies. Similarly, Arjuna killed King Bhagadatta by fraudulent means, when Bhagadatta lost his vision in the battleground.

Both of these actions were carried out under the supervision and advice of Krishna who explained in Bhagavad Gita the tenets of dharma in detail and how these actions came under dharma and not adharma—if they had to resort to unfair means to defeat the people who were the followers of adharma then these actions did not qualify as unethical in war.

An unfair act by Yudhishthira, supported by all the Pandavas except Arjuna, was when he sacrificed Abhimanyu by allowing him to enter the Chakravyuha. Knowing that he was only a child of thirteen years and had no knowledge of how to come out of the Chakravyuha, Yudhishthira let him enter it in Arjuna's absence. Considering that all the decisions were finally approved by Yudhishthira, and that there were other capable warriors in the army who could have shown their mettle in the field, this act of ignorance led to Abhimanyu's demise.

However, sending Abhimanyu to penetrate the Chakravyuha was the only alternative they had since nobody else knew how to do it, except Arjuna, who was battling in another part of the field at that time. Moreover, Yudhishthira made sure that all the great warriors in his army were behind Abhimanyu as he led them through the Chakravyuha. Even though they did follow him, the Kaurava army succeeded in trapping them in such a manner that Abhimanyu got isolated inside and was unable to return.

Arjuna, with Krishna's assistance, deceived Jayadratha and killed him. Jayadratha was one of the main people responsible for Abhimanyu's death. Knowing that Arjuna would kill him to avenge his son's death, the Kauravas protected him in the battlefield. Arjuna had vowed to kill him before sunset that very day, failing which he would jump into a pyre he had created for himself. The Kauravas decided to keep Jayadratha hidden till sunset, after which Arjuna would have to kill himself for having failed. As the time for sunset neared, Krishna created an artificial eclipse by hiding the sun with his Sudarshan Chakra. Jubilant that Arjuna had lost the wager, Jayadratha came out to mock him. At that very moment, Krishna brought back his discus and Arjuna shot an arrow to decapitate him. Even though it is evident that Krishna was the mastermind behind most of the treacheries in the war, it cannot be denied that the Pandavas were the perpetrators of those treacheries.

However, it cannot be forgotten that Jayadratha was an immoral person who had outraged Draupadi's modesty. This was one of the reasons why the Pandavas were so eager to kill him in the battlefield. Moreover, resorting to unfair means was absolutely fine at this point where the fundamentals of dharma had been diluted to such an extent that neither of the armies were following it. Krishna was the one who helped the Pandavas capture Jayadratha by faking the sunset with his Sudarshan Chakra, thus getting implicated in this misdeed.

Another incident that shows that winning the war meant everything to the Pandavas was when they sacrificed Ghatotkacha, the son of Bhima and Hidimbaa, to save themselves from Karna. Ghatotkacha was summoned by Bhima to fight on the Pandavas' side in the battle of Kurukshetra. Invoking his magical powers, Ghatotkacha wreaked great havoc in the Kaurava army. In particular, after Jayadratha's death on the fourteenth day of the battle, when the battle continued past sunset, his powers proved most effective. At this point, having been badly beaten by Ghatotkacha's attacks, Duryodhana appealed to Karna to use his divine weapon called the Vasavi Shakti. The Vasavi Shakti had been granted to

Karna by Indra, but under the condition that Karna could only use it once. Karna had been saving it for his battle with Arjuna, but he realized that he had no choice and hurled the weapon at Ghatotkacha. Fatally wounded, Ghatotkacha flew into the air and made his body grow into a gigantic size, so when he fell to the ground he crushed one akshauhini[8] of the Kaurava army.

I do not see a reason to justify the selfishness of the Pandavas here, considering that they never gave Ghatotkacha the rights and the respect he deserved as the first child born to them. They could have justified it by saying that Ghatotkacha came to them for helping rather than the other way around. Therefore, any casualty as a result of the war was unpredictable and undesired.

The Pandavas plotted to murder their teacher who trusted them more than his own son. Knowing that it would be impossible to defeat an armed Drona, Krishna suggested a plan to the Pandavas to disarm their teacher. Krishna suggested that Bhima kill an elephant named Ashwatthama and make it seem to Dronacharya that he had killed Dronacharya's son Ashwatthama. After killing the elephant, Bhima loudly proclaimed that he had killed Ashwatthama. Disbelieving him, Drona approached Yudhishthira, aware of Yudhishthira's firm adherence to dharma and honesty. When Dronacharya asked for the truth, Yudhishthira responded with the cryptic 'Ashwatthama is dead. But I am not certain whether it is a human or an elephant.' Krishna also knew that it was not possible for Yudhishthira to lie outright. On his instructions, the other warriors blew trumpets and conch shells, raising a tumultuous noise in such a way that Dronacharya only heard that 'Ashwatthama was dead', but could not hear the latter part of Yudhishthira's reply and thus, an aggrieved Drona put down his weapons.

This allowed Dhrishtadyumna to kill an unarmed and unprepared Drona.

Drona's killing was again orchestrated on Krishna's advice, and the events that took place were all a part of the plan to bring down Drona, who was otherwise invincible. The same justification applies here as well that the Pandavas had to resort to unethical means in the war to bring down the supporters of adharma. Even after being asked to lie, Yudhishthira did not speak an outright lie. When he blurted out the truth in the latter part of his sentence, Krishna made sure that the trumpets and horns were blown so loudly that Drona could not hear the rest of it.

At last, Duryodhana's death was also a result of unfair means of warfare. At the end of the war, the Pandavas and Krishna made him an offer that he might pick any of the Pandava brothers to fight with, one-on-one, with a weapon of his choice, and that if he defeated that Pandava, Duryodhana would be deemed the victor of the war. Duryodhana picked his arch-enemy Bhima over the other Pandava brothers whom he could have effortlessly overwhelmed with his skill at fighting with the mace. In the fight that followed, at last Bhima struck Duryodhana in his thighs. This proved to be a fatal blow for Duryodhana who was left to die on the battlefield. This was an unethical move by Bhima, as according to the ethics of warfare hitting below the waist was not allowed.

The killing of Duryodhana was not just a coincidence. Bhima had vowed that he would strike Duryodhana's thighs, since in the past Duryodhana had asked Draupadi in the court to come sit on his thighs. Krishna, knowing well that Duryodhana's thighs were vulnerable, reminded Bhima of his vow that as a Kshatriya, Bhima must hit him on his thighs as promised.

In conclusion, the complex notion of dharma, as defined in the Mahabharata, leaves not just us but even the Pandavas' descendants, agonizing over questions of what is good and bad. Janamajeya, the son of Parikshit (Arjuna's grandson), organizes a ritual to sacrifice all the snakes in his kingdom to avenge the death of his father who was killed by a snake. He is stopped midway in this ritual by Astika, the nephew of the king of the Nagas. Astika explains to Janamajeya that his great-grandfather Arjuna burnt a forest to clear land for his kingdom. The forest was the home of many Nagas (serpents) who were left homeless. The killing of Parikshit was to avenge the wrong done to the Nagas. He points out to Janamajeya that sacrificing more Nagas was only perpetuating the cycle of revenge and violence. The sacrifice would create more orphans, who would be thirsty for the blood of Janamajeya and his descendants. When Janamajeya seeks to justify his action by calling it a measure of justice, Astika responds that what the snake did to his father was also an act of justice. And that it will become the refrain of the Naga orphans, who, in future, would avenge the wrongs done to them. Confused at this thought, Janamajeya hesitantly asks him if justice was not on the side of the Pandavas in the Kurukshetra. Astika tells him that the war was only about dharma, and not about justice. Dharma is not about defeating others but conquering one's self. This somewhat elusive and complex thought is what the Mahabharata leaves us with. Perhaps one thing that it says clearly, is the need to overcome our ideas of self-righteousness, and accept the world in all its complexity, and to always try and see the legitimate claims of justice by those whom we fight against.

However, questions of dharma are not what concern us in this book. Rather it's an inquiry about whether we can establish a connection between the actions of the characters in this epic with their personality dispositions using modern methods of psychology. While clearly the actions of the Kauravas and the Pandavas are not exactly the same, but show close similarities, where the end means everything and the process means nothing. Despite apparent similarities in actions, these two sides are treated entirely differently. Whereas, the Kauravas' actions are entirely villainized, the Pandavas received justifications for all their evil actions. In the next section, I present the justifications in the epic for the evil actions of the Pandavas presented so far.

The Justifications

This section examines the justifications provided in the epic for the Pandavas' seemingly evil actions. The text categorizes these actions into three kinds: those that are the 'need of the hour', those that are based on 'dharma', and those that establish 'dharma'. Here, I consider some of the Pandavas' actions that were discussed in the previous section that fit into these categories.

While Yudhishthira's outburst at Kunti for putting Bhima in danger by sending him to kill Baka at Ekachakrapura clearly appears to be a sign of his neurotic and selfish behaviour, the epic provides a justification for his anger. The Mahabharata presents Yudhishthira's actions as a momentary lapse and not as indicative of his general disposition. For instance, during the same dialogue, we see that Yudhishthira is more concerned with defeating the powerful contemporary agents of 'adharma,' such as Duryodhana and the other Kauravas, than with fighting for smaller social issues that may risk Bhima's life.

Further, while the Pandavas' decision to marry Draupadi collectively appears to be a questionable and manipulative act, the Mahabharata presents this not only as a sign of the Pandavas' unity and political shrewdness, but also as an action befitting the Kshatriyas of the time. The text highlights the precarious situation of the Pandavas—whose lives were in constant danger from Duryodhana and the other Kauravas—and underlines their need for a powerful ally in Drupada. Furthermore, they had to remain united to take on the forces of the Kauravas. Yudhishthira had to ensure that there wouldn't be any dissention among the Pandavas regarding Draupadi.

The Mahabharata further appreciates Yudhishthira's decision as one made with astute foresight that successfully unites the Pandavas against adharma.

Although there is no moral justification for Yudhishthira's behaviour when he manipulates Shalya into vowing to support the Pandavas against the Kauravas, the Mahabharata depicts this act merely as battleground strategy. The epic treats this move as an ordinary attempt to confuse and lure the enemy's alliance, since it did not violate the rules of the war.

Similarly, while the Pandavas' burning of Laakshyagriha kills six innocent people, harms countless animals, and brings massive destruction to the environment, the epic justifies this abhorrent act as an attempt to survive in a harsh and unjust world. And ultimately, as the epic says, the Pandavas had a goal to save dharma.

While Bhima's childhood bullying could have left the readers unsympathetic towards the character, the text presents his behaviour as innocent and playful, causing no permanent harm to the Kauravas. Yet, the text ignores the harm bullying can do to the self-esteem of a young prince and his brothers, especially during an adolescence that is fiercely competitive. While this is not a justification for Duryodhana's attempt to kill Bhima, it highlights the text's deliberate and biased presentation of its characters.

Although abandoning a new mother and her infant child is an act that is universally considered immoral—both today and in the ancient setting of the Mahabharata—the epic presents us with some dharmic justifications for the behaviour. Kunti somehow assures Hidimbaa that Bhima leaving her and their infant in the jungle will be beneficial for everyone involved. She further convinces Hidimbaa that her children are in a precarious position; she explains that she is a fugitive, along with her children, and that they are escaping an assassination bid. She says that they are badly in need of shelter and comfort, and are living in seclusion in order to save and establish dharma.

Where Arjuna's unwarranted jealousy towards Eklavya and Karna is concerned, the Mahabharata again protects the image of the Pandavas. It is mostly silent about Arjuna's disdain for Ekalavya and Karna's skill and acumen, presenting Ekalavya and Karna as victims of the rigidity of gurus and gurukuls. We cannot know whether the text's silence on the Pandava's jealousy is intentional or not. Instead, the epic blames Drona for being insecure about Ekalavya's skills and dedication.

Further, it is worth paying close attention to Arjuna's initial gentle rejection and subsequent acceptance of Ulupi's and Chitrangada's sexual advances. While Arjuna first denies their advances based on his observation of Brahmacharya, his eventual acquiescence is presented as Kshatriya dharma—moral responsibility of a warrior. This is contradictory, but justified by the text, which goes out of its way to establish the Pandava's heroism.

The epic also presents Arjuna's kidnapping of Subhadra as a part of Krishna's meticulous plan, given that Balarama wanted to marry her to his disciple, Duryodhana. Similarly, several other behaviours discussed in this chapter, which appear unfair and sometimes unethical, are justified by the text either as dharma and or as act ordained by Krishna. Krishna in the Bhagavad Gita explains the tenets of dharma and how certain actions come to fall under dharma and not adharma—resorting to unfair means to defeat the followers of adharma is not unethical, he explains.

While the epic provides dharmic justifications for almost all of the Pandavas' unethical behaviour, no such explanation is afforded to Duryodhana or any other Kaurava. While some of Duryodhana's behaviour is clearly immoral, the text's treatment of him compared to its treatment of the Pandavas clearly betrays a biased presentation.

4

DRAUPADI

A Critical Catalyst to Duryodhanization

A larger than life character with an extraordinary story, Draupadi can be interpreted in many ways. She is popularly understood as a woman too independent for her times. A strong, thinking individual who stands her ground and argues for herself, even while being married to five men. But she is also controlled by the situations around her—for one, Draupadi becomes a willing gift to the Kuru household. She is the mediator in her father's plan to kill Drona and only a pawn to her in-laws, who want her father's clan to fight for them in the battle of Kurukshetra.

Draupadi is a copper-toned beauty born of fire. Fiery, gorgeous and strong-willed, Draupadi is born (or reborn) as a result of her father's prayer for revenge against his enemies, and, therefore, personifies this quality throughout her life. We see this most clearly in her burning passion for revenge against the Kauravas, who tried to disrobe her in a full assembly hall and in the presence of her five husbands. Draupadi's oath—that she would only tie her long tresses when they were dipped in Dusshasana's blood—encapsulates her vengeful personality. Her anguish at being disrobed and humiliated in the Kaurava court leads her to curse their entire country—a country where women are reduced to such ignominy will never prosper, she says. However, the epic does not discuss Draupadi's perspectives or feelings when she is asked to enter a polyandrous marriage with five brothers. It is possible that, were she given a choice, she might have objected; however, for reasons the text does not explain, she says nothing.

The fire-born princess rejects Karna, the son of the Sun God, because he was raised by a low-caste man. Karna is bestowed with all the qualities that Draupadi wishes to have in her husband. Still, instead of choosing him, the princess of Panchal marries Arjuna and, eventually, his four brothers as well. However, what's ironic is that her otherwise virtuous husbands, place her as wager in a game of dice against the Kauravas. In addition, none of her mighty husbands come to her rescue when the Kauravas try to disrobe her in public. When she meets a sage, Vyasa, before her swayamvara in order to know her future, he warns her of three significant moments in her life that she needs to be careful about. He warns her to hold back her questions in the first instance, hold back her laughter in the second, and hold back her curse in the final. We all know what happened. Draupadi fails to control her reactions on all three occasions and thus fulfils the prophecy.

The catalytic incident is the episode in which she insults Duryodhana at her palace. When the people of Hastinapur attend the rajasuya yajna in Indraprastha, Duryodhana and his entourage go out to explore the palace of illusions, where Draupadi lives. Entering the palace, Duryodhana encounters a courtyard divided into two parts. While the surface of one part appears to ripple like the surface of a lake, the surface of the other part appears to be solid, like granite flooring. But when Duryodhana attempts to step on the solid half of the courtyard, he finds himself waist-deep in water, drenched from head to toe. When Draupadi and her maids see this from their balcony, they are amused. Draupadi jokes, 'andhasya putra andhaha', which means 'a blind man's (referring to Dhritarashtra) son is blind.'[1] Duryodhana, however, does not find the joke funny and is insulted by the teasing. (Some sources say that Draupadi's blind man joke is only a later addition.)

In some versions of the Mahabharata, Bhima, Arjuna, Nakula and Sahadeva also witness Duryodhana's fall and laugh at him along with their servants. Duryodhana is only further insulted by this, stoking his hatred for the Pandavas.[2]

Yudhishthira's game of dice with Shakuni, in which, having lost everything else, he bets and loses his wife Draupadi, is often considered to be the most important moment in the Mahabharata. Regarded as the incident that sets off the war of Kurukshetra, it also demonstrates Draupadi's fierce bravery and brilliance. The episode begins, when together with his maternal uncle Shakuni, Duryodhana conspires to call the Pandavas to Hastinapur and win their kingdoms in a game of dice. The plan's architect, Shakuni, has a dice that never disobeys his will. The rules are simple: Shakuni and Yudhishthira would play dice until one person loses all of their wealth, the only caveat being that one can stake only that which he can claim as his own. As the rigged game proceeds, Yudhishthira gradually loses all his material wealth. He goes on to put his brothers at stake, and, expectedly, loses them to Shakuni. Finally, he put himself on stake as well, and loses yet again, making all the Pandavas servants to the Kauravas. But for Duryodhana, the Pandavas' humiliation is not yet complete. He prods Yudhishthira to wager Draupadi, luring him with the prospect of winning everything back. Inebriated by the game, Yudhishthira, to the horror of everybody present, puts Draupadi at stake for the next round. Again, Shakuni wins.

Draupadi is horrified to hear that she was placed as a bet in the game, and is now Duryodhana's slave. She questions Yudhishthira's right to put her at stake—after all, while he had lost his autonomy to Duryodhana, she was still a queen. She refuses to present herself in court, angering Duryodhana, who commands his younger brother, Dusshasana to go bring her, forcefully if he must. Dusshasana finds and drags Draupadi to court by her hair.[3] Then deciding to appeal to the elders at the court, Draupadi repeatedly challenges the legality of Yudhishthira's wager. The power structure is exhibited by Draupadi. She now comprehends the position of her spouses and her wretched condition. She hardly waits for others to stretch a helping hand to her. As a queen, she dominates the scene, usurping the power of her husbands. Her brilliant mind boldly enquires the Kuru elders about dharma: 'Tell me, members of this sabha, answer me: what do you think, have I been won or not won, tell me, O lords of the earth?'[4]

After being disrobed by the Kauravas during gambling, Draupadi feels lost and abandoned: in her moment of need, no one, not even her husbands, had helped her. Even as the Kauravas continued to throw insults at her, none of the elders had helped Draupadi, despite her pleas. At the hall, enraged by the insults, Draupadi takes a vow to never oil or tie her hair until it is washed in Dusshasana's blood. Her vow scares everyone present: the king Dhritarashtra requests Draupadi to calm down and frees the Pandavas from their bondage. But Draupadi never ties her hair again and her open hair serve as a constant reminder of the insult she endured.

We see from these incidents that Draupadi's sense of pride and esteem remain unconquered even in the direst of circumstances. After the impotent silence of the brave protectors of dharma, some soft protests from the ordinary, and a miracle, Draupadi is finally defended. Bhima roars with rage, 'I take an oath to tear open the chest of the molester Dusshasana in battlefield and drink his blood.' The oath changes everything. The blind Dhritarashtra, so far enjoying the gambling and Draupadi's humiliation, calls her his most virtuous daughter-in-law, and offers to fulfill her wishes. As the blind king intervenes on behalf of his wayward sons, he grants Draupadi three boons. For her first wish, she asks for her hapless husbands to be set free from bondage. For her second, she asks for the restoration of all the wealth that the Pandavas had lost in the game of dice. She does not, however, claim a third wish—it is beneath a Kshatriya to ask for more than two favours, she says. Her rejection of the third boon could also have been her way of ensuring that the Pandavas realize, that despite all the humiliation she endured, she was the one that saved them. Despite everything, at the end of this episode, Draupadi has the courage, the presence of mind and the wit to plant a final kick at those assembled. In words dipped in sarcasm, she departs with a clever remark, which puns on 'duty':

> One duty remains, which I must now do. Dragged by this mighty hero, I nearly forgot, I was so confused. Sirs, I bow to all of you, all my elders and superiors. Forgive me for not doing so earlier. It was not all my fault, gentlemen of the Sabha.[5]

Why was there a change in Dhritarashtra's attitude after Draupadi's threat? Was it because of the miracle that covered Draupadi with unending yards of cloth or was it Bhima's bloodthirsty pledge? Vidura, the most knowledgeable man present at the assembly, foresees the danger awaiting the Kauravas as a result of Bhima's oath.

Vidura realizes that Bhima's anger is about to change the course of history. Later, when Bhima kills Dusshasana, he brings his blood to Draupadi. She is finally able to tie her hair again.

During the Pandavas' exile, the stubborn Panchali follows her husbands to the forest, leaving her sons in the custody of Subhadra. She does this to make sure that the Pandavas never forget their humiliation and return to seek vengeance after the exile is over. When Yudhishthira opts for peace, it is Draupadi who persuades him to take up arms against the Kauravas and avenge her humiliation in the Dyuta sabha. Throughout their thirteen years of exile, Draupadi does not let her husbands forget how they were deceitfully deprived of their kingdom. After their exile is over, when she learns that her husbands are opting for peace, she is furious. She urges them to take up arms, reminding them that her hair will not be tied until it is washed with the blood of the villain who pulled it.

When Krishna visits Draupadi, she pours out her heart to him; holding up her thick glossy hair and with tearful eyes, she urges Krishna to remember her tresses when he negotiates for peace with the Kauravas. She exhorts that he is bound fourfold to protect her: 'For four reasons, Krishna, you are bound to protect me ever: I'm related, I'm renowned, I'm your sakhi and you rule over all.'⁶ In the event, that even Krishna chooses not to help her, she declares that her five sons, led by Abhimanyu, would avenge her alongside her father and her brothers. Krishna cannot say no to her—he promises to annihilate her tormentors. 'Consider those you disfavor as already dead! . . . The Himavant hills may move, the Earth shatter in a hundred pieces, heaven collapse; my promise stands . . . You will see your enemies killed.'⁷

Death dances its naked tandava like never before. Hundreds of thousands perish every day in the eighteen-day war. Brothers kill brothers, fathers kill sons, uncles butcher nephews, nephews slay uncles, masters and disciples eliminate one another. And strangers massacre strangers. The wails of mothers, daughters, sisters, wives and children pierce the skies. Jackals and vultures tear apart the flesh of the slain men and the dead bodies of animals. Ghouls and cannibals dance in devilish delight and feast on the slaughtered.

Another aspect of the Mahabharata that highlights Draupadi's vengeful nature is Bhima's unconditional love for his wife. Even though Draupadi always favours Arjuna, Bhima is always there to support her. It is Bhima who is most furious during her humiliation, vowing to kill Dusshasana and bring Draupadi his blood—a vow he manages to uphold before the Mahabharata ends. In the Virata Parva, the chapter of the epic describing the final year of the Pandavas's forest exile, we discover the ways in which Draupadi uses her husbands' different personalities to her advantage. In this chapter, the Pandavas and Draupadi are forced to live in disguise as servants in the palace of King Virata. When Virata's loutish brother-in-law, Keechaka, publicly molests Draupadi, who is the queen's handmaiden, Yudhishthira, witness to his wife's humiliation, refuses to help. Be prudent, he says to her, we cannot risk to be discovered till the year is over. Draupadi is not angry with him—Yudhishthira had behaved predictably. When even King Virata does not take any action, she goes to the powerful Bhima, who, when goaded enough, would do whatever Draupadi asks him to. At Draupadi's behest, Bhima secretly kills Keechaka.

On their final journey before ascending to heaven, Draupadi is the first to fall down. Again, it is Bhima who first turns to reach out to her. Yudhishthira, does not, asserting that she cannot ascend to heaven because her love is prejudiced towards Arjuna. But even her favourite, Arjuna, had several other wives, and had a preference for Subhadra. Bhima, on the other hand, was probably the most devoted lover and husband that Draupadi had. He was the first to take bloodcurdling oaths at the Kuru court, vowing to smash Duryodhana's thighs and to drink Dusshasana's blood. Draupadi knew of the passion Bhima felt for her and made good use of it. Whenever she needed something done, be it large (like punishing Keechaka) or small (like acquiring the thousand-petal lotus), she relied on Bhima. She well understood the psychology of her men and motivated them accordingly.

Another of Draupadi's controversial actions that led the Kuru dynasty to its downfall, occurs when Ghatotkacha visits his father's kingdom for the first time. As Ghatotkacha prepares to leave for Indraprastha, Hidimbaa tells him that he should first pay obeisance to his father, then to Krishna, then to Vyasa, and then to Yudhishthira, and that he must not bow to anyone else. His mother also tells him that he has been anointed the king of Indraprastha forest, and as such was like a god to the humans there. As a result of these conversations, Ghatotkacha does not pay respect to Draupadi on his mother's orders. Draupadi is humiliated and shouts at him; she is Yudhishthira's queen, and the daughter of a Brahmin king, she says. How dare he disrespect her at his wicked asura mother's behest in the august assembly of elders, sages and kings? She curses him a short life, dooming him to be killed without a fight—a great dishonour for a Kshatriya. The curse comes true in the battlefield.

Another example of Draupadi's dominant and fierce character is the condition on which she agrees to be the common wife: she would share her household with no other woman. In other words, disregarding popular practice of the times, the Pandavas could not bring their other wives to

Indraprastha. Only Arjuna succeeded in bringing one other wife, Krishna's sister, Subhadra.

Draupadi is often referred to as 'Nathavathi Anathavat', which translates to 'husbanded yet unprotected', a title which expresses her plight of having five husbands, but none willing to protect her. She always has a certain air of loneliness about her. When she pours her heart out to Krishna, she laments that, 'No husband have I, nor son, nor brother. So much so, O Madhusudana, that even you are not mine.'[8]

Draupadi's hidden love for Karna has drawn the attention of many writers. This secret, though not mentioned in many versions of the epic, is considered to be an important episode in many folk renditions of the Mahabharata and is sometimes referred to as the 'Jambul episode (Jambhul Akhyan)'. According to a legend from the Mahabharata, during the thirteenth year of the Pandavas' exile, Draupadi plucks a ripe rose apple, or jambul, from a tree. No sooner does she do this that Lord Krishna appears to stop her from eating it. He informs her that the ripe fruit she is holding was supposed to be the fruit with which the Sage Amitra will break his twelve-year fast. Not finding the fruit in its place, the sage would unleash his wrath on the Pandavas.

Lord Krishna also reveals a way to avoid this problem. In order for the Pandavas to be safe, each one of them must speak only the truth. Saying this, he takes them to the tree and places the fruit under it, asking each one of them to reveal all their secrets. On doing this, the fruit will rise and rejoin the tree of its own accord. One by one, as the Pandavas and Draupadi reveal their truths, the fruit inches up the tree slowly.

At last, Draupadi professes her love for the Pandavas, and reveals the role she played in their present situation. But the fruit doesn't move, and Krishna surmises that she is hiding something. With great trepidation, Draupadi looks into the eyes of her husbands and admits that she wishes she had married Karna—she would have saved herself from misery, she says. This shocks all her husbands, but none of them say anything. The fruit returns to the branch of the tree and all is well with the sage. The Pandavas got the message: in spite of being brave, they had failed their wife when she needed them the most.

Some writers would like us to believe that Draupadi was the epitome of patience, compassion and truth. She was bold, intelligent and argumentative—a champion of morality, who always raised her voice to criticize its defaulters. But unlike many other mythological heroines, Draupadi is not a goddess. Like a human, she is prone to error and fits of temper. She rejects Karna in her swayamvara and humiliates him for his lowly birth. She also mocks Duryodhana for slipping and falling in her palace courtyard. She seeks revenge and utters words of contempt. She takes a vow to not tie her hair until it is washed with Dusshasana's blood. She gloats about the death of her enemies. She curses and clenches her fists in rage. She is not perfect like a god, but she is real like humans. Her troubles too are more human.

Draupadi is perhaps the most complex and controversial female character in Hindu literature. On one hand, she can be womanly, compassionate and generous, and on the other, she can wreak havoc on those who wrong her. She is never ready to compromise on either her rights as a daughter-in-law or on the rights of the Pandavas, her husbands. She secretly vows that she will, one day, avenge the injustice committed against her and her father. And does so by igniting the spark of revenge in the hearts of the Pandavas. If the Mahabharata is an intricately woven saga of hatred and love, bloodshed and nobility, courage and cowardice, beauty and gentleness, victory and defeat, then Draupadi is its shining jewel, casting the shadow of her towering personality over the epic poem and the all-destroying war it describes.

Draupadi first entered the Pandavas' life with the purpose of ending the Kuru clan, ensuring the occurrence of the great war and, during her lifetime, she had many reasons to reinforce that vow. There are several moments in the text, in which Draupadi plays a critical role in keeping the Pandavas in the great war. We can comfortably conclude, then, that the purpose of her life was to fulfil her primary (ending Kuru clan) and secondary (regarding Duryodhana and his younger brother) vows—vows that certainly led to *Duryodhanization*.

V

SOME VAGUE INDUCTIVE
REASONING AND GENERALIZATIONS

In the previous chapters, I've discussed several factors that lead to Duryodhanization. Duryodhana's entire life is an evidence of the role of genetic inheritance in Duryodhanization: his actions and behaviours exhibit clear links with the negative personality dispositions of his ancestors. Clearly, literature review shows that Duryodhana took after his forefathers, and his subsequent Duryodhanization is a natural corollary of his genes.

Another factor causing Duryodhanization is the manner in which Duryodhana is presented in the epic. While the text provides dharmic justifications for the Pandavas' apparently evil actions and behaviours, no such justification is given for those of Duryodhana. This bias in favour of the Pandavas presents them as heroes who need a villain in order to engage the text's readers.

There exist several historical and contemporary academic debates centered on the Pandavas' evil behaviour. While some scholars are in favour of and defend their actions, others reproach and criticize them. In general, however, these debates largely come out in support of the Pandavas. Surprisingly, there are no academic debates about Duryodhana's behaviours, and nearly all discourses present Duryodhana's negative actions as justifications for the Pandavas' similar, retaliatory ones.

The theories regarding the development of a villain that are laid out in the introduction of this book—namely, genetic inheritance, parochialism, ethnocentrism, orientalism, and the Pygmalion approach—all apply to Duryodhana's characterization. However, can these findings be generalized?

In this chapter, I explore the possibility of generalizing the proposition of this book. Here, I present the Duryodhanization of three notorious historical figures, chosen at random to avoid controversies. These figures are Dhana Nanda, the last ruler of the Nanda dynasty, Aurangzeb, from the lineage of the Mughals in India, and Adolf Hitler, who needs no introduction. All three of them are widely acknowledged to be historical villains and, in my opinion, raise the least debate over their villainy.

Dhana Nanda

The Nandas, who usurped the throne of the Shishunaga dynasty, were of low-caste origin. Some sources state that the founder of the dynasty, Mahapadma, was the son of a Shudra mother; others say that he was born of the union of a barber with a courtesan. Curiously enough, the Nandas were one of the biggest dynasties of northern India belonging to a non-Kshatriya caste, until the arrival of the Rajput dynasties, a thousand years later. As elaborated later, there also appears to have been a strange reversal of roles during this era, as the religious teachers of this period were of Kshatriya origin and some of the kings were Brahmins.

The Nandas are sometimes described as the first empire builders of India. They inherited the large kingdom of

Magadha and wished to extend it to even more distant frontiers. To this purpose, Mahapadma Nanda built a vast army, comprising 20,000 cavalry, 2,00,000 infantry, 2000 chariots and 3000 elephants. But the Nandas never had the opportunity to use this army against the Greeks, since Alexander's campaign terminated in Punjab. The army was later inherited by Mahapadma Nanda's son, Dhana Nanda. Not much is known or has been written about Dhana Nanda's mother, other than the fact that she was a low-caste woman called Shunda.

Dhana Nanda is said to have been addicted to hoarding treasure, amassing riches to the amount of eighty *kotis* (small godowns). He even buried some of the treasures he had acquired in a rock that lay in the bed of Ganges. Levying taxes on skins, gums, trees and stones, amongst other common items, he amassed further riches, which he hid similarly. Professor Nilakanta Sastri points out an interesting reference to the 'very famous' Nandas 'victorious in war, who having accumulated treasure first in beautiful Pataliputra hid it in the waters of the Ganges.'[1] Land taxes also became a substantial source of revenue for the treasury. The land was fertile, yielding rich harvests, and the tax could therefore be quite high. The Nandas adopted a methodical system of tax collection by making use of regularly appointed officials as part of their administrative system. The treasury was continually replenished, the wealth of the Nandas increasing. The Nandas also built canals and laid out irrigation projects, which made it seem possible to build an imperial structure based on an essentially agrarian economy. But further development by the Nandas was cut short by Chandragupta Maurya, the young adventurer who usurped the Nanda throne in 321 BC It was under the Mauryas, therefore, that this imperial idea found expression.

The accumulation of an enormous amount of wealth, to which all our authorities bear witness, probably implies a good deal of financial extortion. It is not surprising that Dhana Nanda, a contemporary of Alexander, was detested by his subjects.

Dhana Nanda, the king whose court the famous teacher and philosopher Kautilya came to, was known not only to be baseborn but was also a miser. Quintus Curtius Rufus reports that Porus, who defeated Alexander, wrote to him that the Nanda king 'was not merely a man originally of no distinction, but even of the very meanest condition. His father was in fact a barber.'[2] His father, Mahapadma Nanda, became the lover of the queen of the country, assassinated the king, and while acting as a guardian to the royal children, put to death. Dhana Nanda inherited this Machiavellian trait of his father and went to considerable lengths to achieve his immoral ends.

On top of his ignoble origins, Dhana Nanda was also hated by his subjects for his avarice. He is said to have committed innumerable crimes—using his power to extort money from the poor and killing thousands in the process. He was not only manipulative and Machiavellian in his approach, but also possessed criminal tendencies that resulted in psychopathic behavior. The arrogant king also insulted the scholar Kautilya, who had come to Pataliputra to share his knowledge, ordering him to leave a feast after he had started eating. Clearly, Dhana Nanda was arrogant and narcissistic, believing himself to be superior than everyone else. The incensed Kautilya vowed not to tie his forelock knot again until he had destroyed the Nanda dynasty, root and branch.

While genetic inheritance appears to play a role in Dhana Nanda's actions and behaviours, it alone does not provide sufficient explanation for his historical characterization.

The *Arthashastra*, the earliest complete work of Indian history, was written by Kautilya, who was insulted in the court of Dhana Nanda and swore to destroy the Nanda dynasty. There is no other written account available that explores the Nanda dynasty as comprehensively as the *Arthashastra*, and it is expected that Kautilya in his work would emphasize the shortcomings of the dynasty. Further, nearly no available text describes Dhana Nanda in a positive manner. Therefore, we need to reevaluate whether the texts that we have available, those that Duryodhanize Dhana Nanda, are completely conclusive.

Aurangzeb

Aurangzeb, the third son of the fifth Mughal Emperor Shah Jahan and his Shia Irani wife Mumtaz Mahal, came to occupy the throne after a long and bitter war of succession. The controversy surrounding Aurangzeb, therefore, is not just limited to the actual years of his reign. Aurangzeb is generally considered to be the last powerful Mughal Emperor—his successors failed to hold the empire together, and it soon broke up into smaller regional kingdoms.

The father

A brief study of Shah Jahan, Aurangzeb's illustrious predecessor, is helpful in developing a better understanding of Aurangzeb himself—some of the son's infamous negative dispositions can also be found in the father.

Shah Jahan, the third son of his father, Emperor Jahangir, became the ruler of the Mughal dynasty after winning an extremely bloody war of succession, in which all his brothers, nephews and male first cousins were put to death (Rizvi, 1987:120).[3] To say the least, Shah Jahan was an extremely ambitious man in all his endeavours.

During his rule, Shah Jahan occasionally used the prevailing Islamic sentiment for political advantage. For instance, during the Bundela Rajput rebellion that occurred in the early part of his reign, Shah Jahan ordered the destruction of the colossal Orcha temple and its idols. Ironically, the Orcha temple was built by one of Jahangir's most loyal mansabdars, Raja Vir Singh Dev. A mosque was constructed on the Orcha temple's site and some rebel Bundelas were forcefully converted to Islam. In addition, as Sri Ram Sharma (1962: 86-87)[4] mentions, in the sacred Hindu city of Benaras, Shah Jahan demolished a few temples by enforcing Shariah restrictions. Shah Jahan thus clearly departed from previous Mughal practices, and set new precedents for further acts of religious violence. He was constantly anxious that the majority Hindu population would overthrow the Mughal dynasty, and his violent actions thus underline his psychopathic and neurotic personality traits.

Shah Jahan, best known to students of Indian history for his unmatched patronage of exquisite architecture, had an equally powerful but less-remembered desire to expand the frontiers of the Mughal Empire. He undertook massive military expeditions to the north and the south. The Mughal scheme to conquer their Timurid ancestral regions in the Uzbek-controlled parts of Central Asia proved to be an expensive failure in terms of both personnel and financial resources—a cost that can be attributed to Shah Jahan's personal and narcissistic ambitions.

The mother

In the Mughal dynasty, marriages were often based on political motives. The Mughals strengthened their position in different regions by forming political alliances through marriage. Mughal women worked behind the scenes in marriage negotiations, guiding emperors and princes towards the most beneficial political unions and welcoming new wives into the complex culture of the women's apartments. For instance, Nur Jahan, Jahangir's last wife, married off her niece, Mumtaz Mahal, to Shah Jahan, and Ladli Begum (her daughter from another marriage) to Shahryar Mirza, the other son of Jahangir, in order to strengthen her own position.[5]

Arjumand Bano Begum, later known as Mumtaz Mahal, was the daughter of Asaf Khan, wazir to Emperor Jahangir and Nur Jahan's brother. During the early years of Shah Jahan's reign, his beloved wife Mumtaz Mahal exerted some pressure in political matters. Even before the accession of Shah Jahan to the throne of Delhi, she had cheerfully followed him in his wanderings and exile, patiently bearing the pains and rigours of life in the forests of Telingaha, Bengal, Mewar and the Deccan. According to J.N. Chaudhary, 'In 1628 AD when Shahjahan ascended the throne [Mumtaz Mahal] occupied the premier position in the harem and the emperor usually consulted her about private as well as state affairs.'[6] She was entrusted with the royal seal. After state documents had been finalized, they were sent to the imperial harem, where Mumtaz would imprint the seal on them. This enabled her to get an insight into the current affairs of the empire, in which she took an active interest.

After Shah Jahan's coronation, Mumtaz Mahal was given powers equivalent to those that her aunt, Nur Jahan, had enjoyed as Jahangir's wife, and far greater personal resources. She may not have had the personal ambition or degree of control over her husband that Nur Jahan had had, but Shah Jahan was perfectly content for her to play an important part in his decision-making.

Indeed, her role grew rapidly, and foreign ambassadors were heard to observe with disdain that public business 'slept until it was referred to her', while the emperor himself was 'governed and wound up at her pleasure'. In an unprecedented division of Muslim sovereignty, even coins were minted in the queen's name, and in an echo of the administrative influence of Nur Jahan and queen Guljar Maryam-Zamani before her, Mumtaz Mahal now began issuing royal edicts in her own name.[7] This increase in power could be attributed to Mumtaz's own political shrewdness— Shah Jahan was clearly smitten by her and she could have used this to manipulate him to her own advantage. This suggests that she likely had some Machiavellian traits, which she deployed to access control and power over political matters.

The son

There is historical evidence to suggest that there were significant similarities between Aurangzeb's behaviour and actions and those of his parents. For example, Aurangzeb's forceful and bloody succession to the throne, in which he, like his father, resorted to killing several of his siblings. The two-year-long succession war between Shah Jahan's four sons has received close attention from various scholars (e.g. Richards, 1993:151-153, Misra, 1993)[8] and has usually been interpreted as an ideological contest. Shah Jahan's eldest son, Dara Shukoh and Aurangzeb are portrayed as being representatives of opposing theology. The other two princes, Shuja and Murad, are accorded relatively insignificant roles.

The heir apparent, Dara Shukoh, who was his father's favourite son, lacked Aurangzeb's formidable military talent. As a result, Shah Jahan had to reluctantly acknowledge that the gifted Aurangzeb was the Mughal Empire's best general; he usually sent Aurangzeb on military expeditions or appointed him to governorships of politically unstable provinces. Such demanding experiences enhanced Aurangzeb's military prowess as well as his reputation as a leader of warriors, all of which further accentuated his narcissism.

Aurangzeb also inherited his brilliant, ruthless and shrewd generalship skills from his father. In his 1935 monograph on Aurangzeb, Faruki[9] points out that only Aurangzeb, by winning victories over the formidable Uzbeks, could have kept the Mughal military prestige intact. Mughal southern expansion was not entirely successful but commendable. Although Shah Jahan's father-in-law, wazir Asaf Khan, had failed to annex the premier Deccan state of Bijapur, Aurangzeb forcefully absorbed the smaller Nizam Shahi kingdom of Ahmadnagar into the Mughal Empire in 1632. Aurangzeb seems to have inherited Shah Jahan's powerful urge to annex the remaining Deccan kingdoms. To assert his superiority, as well as his control over his territories, Aurangzeb did not hesitate in committing atrocities against the residents of the conquered regions, suggesting that he inherited his father's narcissistic and psychopathic disposition.

Aurangzeb is often blamed for his religious rigidity and intolerance, and scholars have noted his use of religion for political gain. For example, Athar Ali (1968:97)[10] provides details of the most important religion based ruling Aurangzeb used: he declared that Gods bestowed more powers to him in comparison to all others he had the right to rule even while his father was still alive, demonstrating his narcissism.

Aurangzeb's decision in April 1679 to impose the hated poll tax, known as the *Jizyah*, on the empire's non-Muslim subjects is usually seen by historians as just one of a series of anti-Hindu measures. It is also regarded as a regressive step, which brought the Akbari tradition of religious tolerance in the Mughal Empire to an end. The re-imposition of the Jizyah some hundred years after its abolition by Akbar seems to suggest that Aurangzeb was trying to mirror the Delhi Sultanate. The Jizyah increased the social distinction between Hindus and Muslims; the former felt discriminated by the Mughal Empire and some violently protested against the state authorities. Saiyid Abbas Ali Rizvi (1987: 183) thinks that Aurangzeb might have believed that Hindu affluence was the cause of local rebellions. As such, the imposition of the Jizyah could be considered an appropriate measure taken to curb the outbreak of revolts by restricting Hindu financial resources. This analysis, which may explain some revolts, fails to account for the majority of rebellions, which were sparked by over-taxation in the first place.

Hallisey (1977)[11] is justified, then, in saying that Aurangzeb's real fault was not his religious, but rather his personal inflexibility. While Aurangzeb is largely perceived to be a Mughal Duryodhana, there is some historical evidence that justifies his villainous behavior. For example, Aurangzeb is generally criticized by many historians for using religion as a rallying call during the succession war, but Rizvi (1987:132)[12] disputes this claim, insisting that both Murad and Shuja abused religious sentiment as a political tool far more than Aurangzeb did. In such a competitive climate, Aurangzeb had to appeal to the Muslim religious establishment without alienating the Hindu Rajput *mansabdars*.

Although primarily an architectural historian, Catherine B. Asher is extremely well versed in Mughal history—she is among the few historians to tackle, without prejudice, the highly controversial topic of temple demolition during Aurangzeb's reign. Her work primarily discusses the demolition of the Keshava Deva temple in Mathura, which Aurangzeb destroyed in retaliation against the Mathura Jat rebellion. Not only were several thousand Mughal troops and imperial *faujdars* killed during the rebellion, the Jats also destroyed the tomb of Aurangzeb's great-grandfather, Akbar, and burnt his remains. For this reason, Asher (1992:253-259)[13] argues that Aurangzeb tore down Hindu temples only in response to large-scale anti-state activities, thus exhibiting his neurotic and psychopathic traits. Aurangzeb also may have viewed temples as the planning grounds for many revolts, further making them the target of his violence.

Historians often associate Aurangzeb with the destruction of a great number of temples. The compiler of the British colonial censuses, William Crooke (1972:112-113)[14] believes that while some temples were indeed cruelly leveled, many myths were created to enhance the sacredness of some temples. Myths suggest that Aurangzeb failed to knock down many of these sacred temples, and his troops were defeated by the supernatural powers of the Hindu deities.

While Aurangzeb was resented by his subjects for re-imposition of the Jizyah tax, there is practically no historical evidence available that explains how the collections under this tax were used. We do not know, then, whether the funds accumulated under the Jizyah were ever put to any specific infrastructural or developmental use at all. Under Aurangzeb's reign, censors were appointed to enforce a strict moral code, and laws were issued against prostitution, gambling, drinking and narcotics. Whether we call such impositions anti-religion (to limited sectors in society) or not, surely this overly moralistic attitude and intolerance highlight Aurangzeb's psychopathic and narcissistic personality along with his Machiavellian traits.

While debates about Aurangzeb will persist, we can conclude that he inherited some of his dispositional characteristics from his parents, and his judgement certainly suffered from parsimonious and bounded rationality. And that is the only purpose of the book.

Hitler

More than fifty years after the end of World War II, Adolf Hitler continues to fascinate us: dozens of biographies and political analyses have been published about him and Nazi Germany in the last few years. The shadow of the Holocaust he created continues to darken the twenty-first century. Adolf Hitler and his Nazi party perpetrated one of history's most evil acts by committing mass genocide and instigating World War II, which led to tens of millions of lives being lost or irreparably damaged. What drove Hitler to act in such a monumentally murderous, horrific, and ultimately self-destructive way?

What do we really know about Hitler's personality? Perhaps the most famous psychological study of Hitler was done by Henry A. Murray, former director of Harvard Psychological Clinic, at the behest of the American OSS during the war.[15] Murray points out that though there is very little information available about Hitler's childhood, he is said to have been sickly and frail. His father was described as 'tyrannical' and physically abusive; according to psychoanalyst Michael Stone, Hitler's father reportedly beat both him and his older brother with a whip regularly, meting out daily whippings to the more rebellious Adolf, who, by the time he turned eleven, 'refused to give his father the satisfaction of crying, even after thirty-two lashes'.[16] Aside from doling out physical punishments, his father had little interest in child rearing.

Here we can begin to see how Hitler as a young boy was physically abused by his father, and confronted with a situation that he could not control, he instead learned to control his own emotions and actions. It could be further suggested that Hitler's hatred for his father fueled his hatred of Jews, who, after his father died when Hitler was fourteen, served as scapegoats for his residual fury.

Hitler, like so many victims of childhood physical or sexual abuse, may have experienced an extraordinary sense of helplessness as a boy. It is frequently this terrifying feeling of total powerlessness in childhood that drives what Nietzsche calls a 'will to power' later in life. As depth psychologist Alfred Adler points out, such tragic circumstances engender 'inferiority feelings', which, in the form of 'increased dependency and the intensified feeling of our own littleness and weakness, lead to inhibition of aggression and thereby to the phenomenon of anxiety'.[17] In turn, this becomes what Adler refers to as 'masculine protest', consisting of a compensatory superiority complex, aggression, ambition, avarice and envy, coupled with constant 'defiance, vengeance, and resentment'.[18] Thus, all of this resulting into narcissistic, neurotic and psychopathic acts or tendencies.

As a result of his father's violent behaviour and abuse, Hitler seems to have identified more with his mother, with whom he was quite close. As such, he may have decided to reject his father's 'masculine' aggression, anger and rage, choosing instead to become more 'feminine' like his mother. This would have rendered him highly susceptible to becoming 'possessed' by his chronically disowned anger, a phenomenon noted by psychoanalyst Erich Fromm, who refers to Hitler's barely controlled and intensely intimidating 'attacks of anger'.[19]

There seems to be no question that Hitler's barely repressed anger, rage and resentment, especially towards his father, fueled much of his destructive behaviour. He may have also harboured some resentment towards his mother, despite their close relationship, for not protecting him from her husband.

Hitler's parents' marriage was not a happy one. Robert G.L. Waite notes that, 'even one of his closest friends admitted that Alois was "awfully rough" with his wife, Klara, and "hardly ever spoke a word to her at home".[20] When Alois Hitler was in a bad mood, he would pick either on his older children or on Klara, even while the children would be watching. Alois' hostility towards his wife could only have added to Hitler's resentment of his father.

When he was older, his father wanted him to seek out a career in the civil service. However, Hitler had become so alienated from his father that he rejected anything that he wanted. He sneered at the thought of a lifetime spent enforcing petty rules. Even though his father tried to browbeat his son into obedience, Hitler did his best to be the opposite of whatever his father wanted.[21]

In 1998, Fritz Redlich developed a psychopathologic profile of Hitler with great care.[22] Reviewing Hitler's family's medical history, which was studded with mental illnesses, Redlich concludes that Hitler's preoccupation with degeneracy and mental illness can be traced to his family; he argues further that historians largely underestimate the role this preoccupation played in shaping Hitler's view of life. He was convinced that he would die early and have insufficient time to realize his ideas. He was also sexually conflicted, and fears of prostitution and syphilis feature prominently in his writings and speeches. Redlich rejects categorically the idea that Hitler had syphilis, but he concludes that he suffered from severe syphilophobia. Syphilis, Hitler believed, was a Jewish disease that was 'transmitted generationally, and destroyed races, nations, and ultimately mankind'. His views on mental illness and sexuality, thus, further demonstrate his neurotic and psychopathic disposition.

Redlich also studied Hitler's paranoid delusions, particularly his belief in the threat of Jewish world domination. Hitler's dominant ego defence was excessive self-projection, which regularly interfered with his evaluation of his adversary's intentions. In addition to highlighting his paranoia, Redlich also identifies the manifestations of Hitler's narcissism: his grandiose behaviour, his tenuous personal relationships, his sensitivity to criticism, and his potential for rage. These two personality characteristics—paranoia and narcissism—together gave shape to Hitler's violent anti-Semitic ideology. Hitler exemplifies the destructive charismatic personality who unifies his wounded people by identifying and attacking an enemy. From the perspective of the big five personality types, Adolf Hitler was a neurotic person.

According to Murray, the adult Hitler was a 'counteractive type', which refers to a person primarily motivated by resentment and revenge that is borne out of past narcissistic wounds and profound feelings of inferiority. Pathological narcissism develops as a compensatory defense against these painful wounds and inferiority complexes. Hitler's personality demonstrated all the signs of pathological narcissism, also known as psychopathic narcissism, and he may have met the modern diagnostic criteria for a narcissistic personality disorder.

Hitler was also known for his personal rigidity, i.e. his inability or refusal to change in any significant way. He described this quality in him in *Mein Kampf*, maintaining that he had developed all his core ideas in Vienna early on in his adult life: 'In this period there took shape within me a world picture and a philosophy which became the granite foundation of all my acts . . . I have had to alter nothing.' His boyhood friend and Viennese companion August Kubizek also singled out rigidity as Hitler's most notable trait. He said:

> The most outstanding trait in my friend's character was, as I had experienced myself, the unparalleled consistency in everything that he had said and did. There was in his nature something firm, inflexible, immovable, obstinately rigid, which manifested itself in his profound seriousness and was at the bottom of all his other characteristics. Adolf simply could not change his mind or his nature.[23]

This inflexibility was expressed in Hitler's life in many forms. Even as an adult, he continued to make the same grammatical and spelling errors that he had made as a child. His daily routine also remained intact, down to its smallest details. When he became chancellor, his daily walks would always follow the same path. He insisted on a fixed seating order for meals, and any deviation resulted in an outburst of anger. A fixed post-dinner routine, consisting of motion pictures and multi-hour Hitler monologues, quickly became monotonous for regular guests.[24]

Hitler's unwillingness to change was the result of his personal insecurity and anxiety. He was tormented by the fear of appearing ridiculous and would not allow himself to be photographed doing anything insignificant, lest it undermine his dignity. He was even disgusted with Mussolini for permitting himself to be photographed in a bathing suit, something Hitler believed a 'great statesman' would never do. Hitler constantly blamed others for his own failures and couldn't bear the thought of making a mistake.

Unable to tolerate being around those who might be considered 'superior' to him, Hitler often surrounded himself with people of inferior intelligence. One exception to this practice was Albert Speer, whose architectural talents were congenial to Hitler's own image of himself as a great architect. Hitler also liked to have men with physical or emotional weaknesses in his presence so that he could ridicule them. His actions betray not only a superiority complex, but also a great ego, clearly underlining his narcissistic personality.

Moreover, Murray, who never actually met or examined Hitler in person, finds that Hitler demonstrated other signs of neurosis towards the end of his four years of military service during World War I, where he developed a case of 'hysterical blindness' and 'mutism', possibly in response to 'shell shock' or what we now call post-traumatic stress disorder. Even earlier, during adolescence, Hitler is said to have developed syphilophobia, a dread of being contaminated by sexual contact with women, which, according to acquaintances, eventually led to sexual impotence. As Führer, Hitler's neuroses persisted and probably worsened, often taking the form of intense episodes of 'emotional collapse' that were characterized by violent bouts of furious screaming and crying. Indeed, Murray accurately identifies Hitler's characterological core of hatred, rage and resentment as the 'mainspring' of his career, describing him diagnostically as a borderline paranoid schizophrenic and hysterical 'megalomaniac'.[25] Indeed, it can be argued that perhaps the major component of Hitler's madness was his immense anger, embitterment and hatred towards his father and, eventually, towards Jewish people and the world at large.

People like Hitler often see themselves as messiahs. This grandiose self-portrait is accompanied by an elevated mood that alternates with periods of despair and emotional outbursts of crying or rage. Such individuals are commonly perceived to be suffering from some type of bipolar disorder. Indeed, much of Hitler's documented behaviour and demeanour appears to be consistent with such a retrospective diagnosis, his mania masking a chronic underlying state of despair, sadness and rage.

Often gifted with the ability to influence and move the masses with their oratory skills and 'messianic' visions, such leaders become the incarnation of the crowd's unspoken needs and cravings. Hitler was able to uniquely mobilize and manipulate the masses with his words, demonstrating his Machiavellian traits.

While the literature clearly shows us that Adolf Hitler possessed all the personality traits that make a villain, there is limited and debatable account available of Hitler's positive traits. This is surprising, because, at the height of his rule, Hitler had a massive following that believed in him. In a political career of nearly two decades, why did no one stop him? Here, I will not propose any theories or explanations that go against popular perceptions—however, as a personality scientist, Hitler's cult following is worrisome. Did Hitler really have no positive traits or is this perception only a parochial development of knowledge?

We have seen then, that Dhana Nanda, Aurangzeb, and Hitler all possessed stark similarities in their personalities. All three historical figures had similar life arcs and modern historiography has treated them similarly as well. It is clear then that they were the Duryodhanas of their times.

CONCLUSION

Radhe was to be released from jail today.

And the calculation of his life continued.

He lost his mother, when, he does not remember. He was, as they say, only a kid. His father died just as his family was going through a financial crisis. Radhe could not repay his father's debt. His house, his iron forge, everything got impounded by the government. For the first time in his thirteen years of living, he had alcohol. In his seventeenth year, he committed a major robbery and escaped. In his twenty-second year, for something similar, he went to jail for the first time—though for only two years. One of Radhe's jail mates got him married to his cousin. They say his behaviour was too elegant for jail, which was all right. In his thirty-fourth year, he thrashed the village chief—why, we don't know. He had come to murder the chief, but instead cut off only his nose and went to jail for the second time in his life, this time for six years.

Between his first and second jail terms he got married to Aru, and had a son, Kichlu.

He remembered his last conversation with his wife, Aru, before he was taken in for the second time.

'Don't worry about me,' said Radhe. 'And listen to me. Kichlu has grown up now, and you cannot deny the fact that *he has the same blood that flows through my veins. I am a thief, a dacoit, a robber. I have the speed of a thief and the shrewdness of a robber. But Kichlu is a fool—he has got your innocence in him, understood? Take care of him. Keep him close to your heart. Make sure that my blood in his veins never boils. Got it?'*

Six years went by and Radhe was released from jail.

When Radhe came out of the jail compound, the sky was brown, bulging with clouds. Far away, the Murna river was roaring with life and rigor. More than ten bullock carts were waiting for the waters to subside so they could cross over to the other side. But the river was overflowing.

All kinds of people were waiting to cross the river, which would bring Radhe closer to his home. Radhe saw among those people a beautiful and voluptuous girl with curious eyes. She, the potter girl, appeared to be in the utmost hurry to cross the river. When there was no sign of the river calming down as night fell, she burst into tears near the plinth of a peepal tree. Radhe was standing in front of her. At first, he could not understand what to say as the girl kept crying.

It started to get darker. The wind slowed down. The people waiting at the bank started dispersing and the crowd became thinner and thinner, until there were very few people left.

Stricken, Radhe kept looking at the potter girl. In his life, he had not faced many delicate situations like this. He stammered while trying to say something sweet to her to sooth and calm her.

'Now get up—that's enough.'

But the potter girl did not get up.

'Are you deaf?' Radhe said harshly, unable to stop himself. 'Do you want to spend the night here under the peepal tree? Absolutely stupid. There is a small temple with a sanctuary nearby. People are taking shelter there. I am heading there too. Join me.' He couldn't fathom the command he had over the potter girl or her willingness to listen.

The potter girl finally got up and walked to the temple. The cloudy evening had spread a morose colour everywhere and in that withering twilight, while looking at the shadow of the potter girl with her head hung low, a thought crossed Radhe's mind again— that she is beautiful and voluptuous. But it went away as it had come.

His mind was elsewhere as he entered the sanctuary. He showed the potter girl a corner and said loudly for everyone to hear, 'Keep sitting here—and if someone has a problem with that then don't hesitate using some really abusive words.'

Then he went and leaned against a nearby pillar. Everyone was busy eating. He looked at the potter girl properly in the light of a grocer's lantern. She was beautiful. She had a mature body but she couldn't have been more than sixteen years old, he guessed. He couldn't see her sparkling teary eyes but thought that she must otherwise be smiling all the time.

He didn't try to fall asleep as soon as he lay down. At first his thoughts did not disturb him much. But soon they began to excite him. With each passing hour his excitement kept growing. He did not know if he was excited to return home or if it was due to his current company. He smoked two or three cigarettes. His broad chest was now warm and his head felt heavy.

Radhe went out and drank local liquor, but only a little.

After coming back to the sanctuary, he stood in a corner, leaning against a wall for a while. His empty eyes kept wandering everywhere. Eventually the cold wind shut his eyes and he slept beside the wall.

When his eyes opened, Radhe saw that someone was sleeping on the floor near him very comfortably.

And when he realized it was the potter girl, he became anxious for a moment. He turned his face away. But that feeling was momentary. He looked at her again, now with determination and arrogance.

She was resting her head on a rock. The wind had shifted her dupatta from her chest and stomach, and my goodness! Her blouse was not in place either! A tiny square silver pendant with a zari around it was lying on her heaving naked chest.

This time, Radhe kept staring at her. He was not able to keep his eyes off her. Slowly, all his thoughts vanished. He was no longer in his senses.

The potter girl was fast asleep. One of her legs was bent over the other. Her right hand fingers lay under her cheeks touching her lips and the left hand was lying like a lifeless snake next to her. He fell asleep again.

When his eyes opened again, the colour and wrinkles on his face had changed. His six-year-long hunger was aroused.

This beauty, this youth and this precious moment on a monsoon night.

And such innocent youth, it was! Radhe had a wicked smile on his face and his eyes narrowed into slits. The heat in his chest was rising. Radhe jumped over the stairwell like a swift cat. He turned around and looked at the sanctuary carefully.

The atmosphere was lethargic, even as his emotions soared. And when his gaze turned to the potter girl, his body shivered with excitement. He became a slave of that gaze.

The potter girl's body lay like flowing water over the rock. Those innocent eyes, those colourful lips! Radhe's evil body took over him and he gave in to it.

The thief's eyes became empty and then full again. Suddenly he felt scared of someone. He straightened up. His body had gotten loose and the wrinkles on his face were gone. He raised his face and looked up, way up. The swinging pendant mesmerized him. Radhe was lost in the pleasure of the beauty of the three worlds that was at the peak of the potter girl's youth. He felt as if a lot had happened, had already happened. He sighed.

The tipsy-tiddley night was finally over. The day had not dawned yet and the west wind had already started blowing.

He was about to leave to get breakfast for both of them.

As he touched her dupatta, the potter girl awakened and sat up surprised. 'Oh my!'

Radhe laughed.

'See, how she was sleeping? I thought I'd cover you with the dupatta . . .' Radhe was unable to say anything else.

The potter girl looked at her condition and quickly stood up, wrapping her dupatta around her, agitated.

'Neither do you want to eat nor do you want to sleep, is it, Uncle?'

'Girl, don't call me Uncle.'

'Okay!' the girl spread her right hand and said, 'As if that's an abusive word? If not Uncle, then what should I call you? Son? And I am Shanti.'

'Call me Radhe.'

'No, Radhe Uncle.'

'Now go sleep!'

'And you?'

'I will get breakfast.'

'Girl, you are naïve. Aren't you afraid?'

'Afraid of what? And if something happens, you aren't too far away, right?'

Abruptly, he put on his turban and left.

He took a while to return with breakfast. The travelers were leaving in their bullock carts. He couldn't spot Shanti anywhere.

He went to wash his hands and face at a well near the temple, when he saw Shanti washing her clothes at the end of a gutter flowing from the well. Radhe walked over to her and asked while laughing, 'Aren't you stupid? Come here, you cannot wash clothes there.'

Shanti, caught by surprise, quickly picked up her clothes, hid them behind her back and looked down.

Radhe saw that her eyes were swollen and red from crying. She had scratches on her cheeks and arms, and was shivering.

Before Shanti could say anything, Radhe snatched her clothes away and saw that there were bloodstains on them, which Shanti was trying to wash. Her blouse was torn in the front and was in shreds.

'Who was that demon?', Radhe yelled, 'Say something! I will break his bones.'

In her response, Shanti started crying and sobbing.

Radhe's eyes were full of fury.

'Did he cut your tongue? Tell me who that son of a pig was.'

Shanti felt ashamed, her eyes darting from left to right, and said—

'Keep your voice low—what had to happen, happened. Why are you broadcasting it now?'

Radhe felt sick and sat on a rock nearby. He started smoking. Shanti looked down and said—

'It happened after you left in the morning. Before I could wake up and rouse the others, someone clamped my mouth shut and held me down with both hands, and he . . . ' She started crying while speaking. 'There were two of them and I . . . I resisted a lot. I thought I would die before letting something like this happen to me—but that's exactly what has happened. I couldn't recognize him—I don't even remember his face. But he was wearing a silk shirt, a ring and one of his little fingers was missing. Bloody demon!'

Radhe was caught in a web of thoughts. He was sitting with clenched fists. 'If only you could have recognized him,' he said, 'I would have gouged out his eyes.'

'What is the point now, Uncle?' Shanti said and stood up. Radhe too got up. For a while, they both didn't say anything. Radhe had felt uncomfortable when she had addressed him as 'uncle', but he did not say anything this time.

'Okay, come now,' Radhe said, 'My house is on the other side of the river, eat and drink something there before you go anywhere.

Shanti followed him but her gait no longer had the lively elegance of a butterfly.

Everyone had crossed the river. Only one bullock cart was left; it was waiting for passengers.

Radhe paid the fare and they got into the cart.

After a while, Shanti said—

'Uncle, I have always been unfortunate.

'My mother died while giving birth to me When I was thirteen, our house was mortgaged. My brother is dead and now my father too is about to die.' She sighed. 'And to top it off, my husband threw me out of the house.'

Radhe was taken aback. He looked into her eyes—there was so much grief in them and yet he asked like a fool, 'What? threw you out? But you are so beautiful!'

'Yes, and playful too. That is what my bad luck is. I am cheerful by nature and never realize when I can be too full of emotions. At my in-laws' and parents' places, all I ever saw was poverty and illiteracy. I think I should control myself. Otherwise, anybody can think of me as anything, and you cannot shut people's mouths, right? But . . . But,' Shanti's eyes filled with tears. 'But I became my own enemy and had to leave my husband's house. People started spreading rumors about me. What I was afraid of eventually happened. My nature betrayed me. My husband got annoyed. I kept laughing. He kicked me out of the house. I . . . I have always been unfortunate.'

Radhe felt miserable. By that time, they had reached the riverbank. He jumped out and Shanti followed him.

'Be careful. Don't go there. There is a bog over there.'

The village was visible now.

'Look, that house with a courtyard and the tall tamarind tree is mine.' Radhe smiled. 'I am returning home after five and a half years.'

'Really? Did you go abroad to earn?

'No' Radhe said, 'I went to jail. Ha ha!' He guffawed. Then he slowed down and started walking beside Shanti. He got tensed again.

'I am a thief, understood. You are not afraid of me, are you?'

'Who? Scared of you?'

Shanti looked at Radhe with tears in her eyes. 'For me, you are not a thief.' And she laughed for the first time that day. Radhe felt happy. He laughed out loud.

'I am a thief, a good one too, understood?'

Meanwhile, they reached his house. The doors were open. Radhe saw there was a horse tied to a tree in his courtyard.

'What's this?' he said, 'A horse in my courtyard! It seems in my absence the king has showered this place with all his wealth.'

Aru came running outside, hearing his voice. 'It's you!' She said, 'I knew this could only be your voice.' Radhe approached his wife and stood next to her.

'You look fine! What is this merriment going on here? Whose horse is this?'

Shanti went and stood behind Radhe quietly.

Aru laughed.

'It's Kichlu's horse—he just crossed the river and came back. Didn't you meet him at the sanctuary on the other side?'

'Where is he anyway?' Radhe became restless.

'He's eating in the kitchen.'

Soon, Kichlu came out of the kitchen, laughing, 'Here I am!' But as soon as he spotted Shanti, his laughter froze and his eyes grew wide in horror.

And when Shanti saw him, she screamed and hid behind Radhe, holding his arm. The bundle of clothes she was holding fell on the ground and the half-washed bloodstained clothes got scattered. As Radhe's eyes fell on them so did his son's, which the former noticed. He also noticed that Kichlu was wearing a silk shirt, a ring, and one of his little fingers was missing.

Radhe gritted his teeth, 'Rascal! Shameless devil!' Before anybody could stop him, he hit his son violently. Kichlu fell down, his mouth bleeding.

'What? What have you done? Have you returned with a bloodthirst?' Aru said as she bent down and covered Kichlu's body like monsoon clouds in the sky.

'What terrible wrong has he done to deserve this?'

Radhe grabbed Aru's hand and pushed her away.

'Ask that pig!'

Kichlu rose up, crossed the porch and ran towards the gate. Shanti fell down at Radhe's feet and cried, 'No-no, let him go, Uncle!'

'Shut up! don't call me Uncle!'

'You returned after so many years and . . . ' Tears streamed down Aru's cheeks. Her voice choked. 'And this precious boy . . . '

'Precious?' Radhe yelled.

'Look at him—he who raped this innocent girl. Whose son is he? Tell me whose drop of blood is he?'

His eyes, which were full of passion, became empty in an instant. The tension on his face vanished. The beautiful moment flashed in front of his eyes—the breeze, the cloudy night, the dupatta, that pendant and that openness full of relief that one wanted to get lost in.

Radhe sat down with a thud. He had never cried before, but today his eyes were wet.

Aru sat beside him and running her fingers through his coarse hair, asked gently—

'I too am asking you the same thing—whose drop of blood is he?'[1]

Whose drop of blood was Duryodhana?

The five dispositional traits—Machiavellianism, narcissism, psychopathy, neuroticism, and sadism— that make up a villain's personality can be easily traced to Duryodhana's ancestors. Figure 1 shows a family tree that maps the DNA transmission in the Kuru clan. While Satyavati exhibits Machiavellianism, narcissism, and neuroticism in several of her actions and behaviours, Shantanu displays narcissism, neuroticism and psychopathy. Similarly, Ambika, Duryodhana's grandmother, also exhibits neurotic and psychopathological tendencies. In fact, Ambika's characterization in the epic clearly indicates her worried and fearsome behaviour.

Further, we can also find traces of the five negative personality traits in Ambika's son, Dhritarashtra. Indeed, the epic provides us with several examples of Dhritarashtra's villainous actions and behaviours. His jealously towards Pandu and his sons, his possessiveness towards the throne, his insecurities about his children, his excessive desire for worldly possessions, and his lusty demeanour are just some of the many behaviours that indicate that Dhritarashtra was indeed a DNA carrier of several negative dispositional traits

Similarly, Duryodhana's mother, Gandhari's actions and behaviours also demonstrate several mixed and villainous characteristics in her personality. For example, the text is ambiguous about her decision to blindfold herself in order to render herself blind like her husband: it is unclear whether she does this to share his experience or to shame and guilt him. In fact, her vow to end the Kuru clan in order to avenge the insult caused to her family by her abduction and forced marriage, also are significant indicators of negative traits in her.

It is evident then that Duryodhana inherits much of his personality from his ancestors. There are many more signs in the text that indicate the role played by family in Duryodhana's inheritance of negative traits. For example, all of his grandparents had difficult married lives. Dyads such as Satyavati–Shantanu, Ambika–Vichitravirya (or Veda Vyasa), and finally, Gandhari–Dhritarashtra all suffered from troublesome marriages.

While we can comfortably conclude that Duryodhana's personality was merely a constellation of the personality traits of his ancestors and the outcome of their disturbed married lives, a new question arises: where did the Pandavas get their heroism from? In theory, the Pandavas should have had personalities like Duryodhana. But clearly, there are stark differences. Despite a shared ancestry and inheritance, the Pandavas' characterization is constructed in opposition to that of Duryodhana. How did the author of the epic justify the Pandavas' heroism against Duryodhana's villainy?

We can find the answer to the above question in Figure 1, which shows that the Pandavas' ancestry is unclear and seemingly obscure. While Duryodhana and the Pandavas have a common family tree till the birth of Pandu, thereafter the Pandavas' lineage becomes hazy. For example, the epic is silent on the identity of the Pandavas' actual fathers. We only know, from the epic, that Pandu took Kunti and Madri along with him to the jungle, where the Pandavas were born. However, with some speculation, we can probably conclude that Pandu was impotent. Then whose children were the Pandavas? Scarce evidence is presented in the epic, which obfuscates who Kunti and Madri niyoged with.

However, our primary inquiry is not about the exact ancestry of the Pandavas. What is interesting, however, is asking why the text chooses to conceal the identities of the Pandavas' real fathers? Was this decision the outcome of smart authorship, simply an after-thought, or careful HARKing?[2]

These questions certainly raise red flags. There is evidence in the epic that suggests the possibility of HARKing. For example, in addition to concealing the identities of the Pandavas' fathers, Kunti's characterization is also very interesting. The text presents Kunti as a strong woman with an independent mind—I called her the DNA disruptor. Noticeably on the other hand, Pandu's second wife Madri is shown to be immature and vulnerable. This difference in characterization probably exists to justify Nakula and Sahadeva's lifelong subordination to the other three Pandavas.

The Mahabharata is a very interesting and seemingly scientifically crafted epic. Its author(s) have attempted to address almost every aspect of a person's life in some form across the long epic. As this book shows, they even discuss and consider genetic inheritance. The Mahabharata is a fascinating study in the creation and development of a character.

Duryodhana is a well-crafted character who performs several villainous actions and behaviours. The epic presents enormous evidence in favour of reading genetic inheritance as the most powerful force in shaping his personality. Additionally, while Duryodhana's characterization firmly roots him as evil, the Mahabharata is less definitive in its portrait of heroes and heroism—they are presented as heroes relative to those around them. For example, the unclear and well-concealed ancestry of the Pandavas, the characterization of Kunti as a strong woman, Draupadi's instigative role, and Bhishma and Drona's indifference, all add to the heroism of the Pandavas. Also, while justifications for the Pandavas' apparently evil behaviour are available in the epic, no such treatment is extended for the villainous actions and behaviours of Duryodhana. While readers are largely allowed to form their own opinions about Duryodhana, the epic certainly attempts to influence how they read him and what conclusions they draw about the Pandavas—a critical element in the process of Duryodhanization.

Finally, Duryodhanization has been adapted into the work of historians and academics and through them by common man. As I discussed in the early chapters of this book, systematic and planned disbursement, development and distribution of knowledge, often leads to a bounded rationality. Though our sample size is only four units—Duryodhana, Dhana Nanda, Aurangzeb and Hitler—phenomenology and a qualitative literature review clearly indicate that the characterization of all four are 'Duryodhanized' in many ways.

Conclusively, then, the Mahabharata leaves us with yet another critical learning—Duryodhanization.

Notes

Introduction

1. The study of the origin of words and the way in which their meanings have changed throughout history.
2. Falsification is a term used by social scientists when they find new evidence to extend an existing theory or propose a new theory.

I The Usual Suspects: Personality Traits Responsible for Villainous Behaviour

1. Saul Kassin, *Psychology* (USA: Prentice-Hall, Inc., 2003).
2. Thomas J. Bouchard Jr. and John C. Loehlin., *Genes, Evolution, and Personality* (Behavior Genetics, Vol. 31, No. 3, 2001).
3. R.C. Nichols, *Homo* (1978): 29, 158.
4. E. Turkheimer, 'Three Laws of Behavior Genetics and What They Mean', *Current Directions in Psychological Science* (2000): 9, 160–64.
5. David Watson, *Mood and Temperament* (New York, NY: Guilford Press, 2000).
6. David Watson, Lee Anna Clark and Auke Tellegen, 'Development and Validation of Brief Measures of Positive

183

and Negative Affect: The PANAS Scales', *Journal of Personality and Social Psychology* 54 (1988): 1063–70.

7. Alike Tellegen, David T. Lykken, Thomas J. Bouchard, Kimerly J. Wilcox, Nancy L. Segal and Stephen Rich, 'Personality Similarity in Twins Reared Apart and Together', *Journal of Personality and Social Psychology* 54 (1988): 1031–39.

8. Lisa M. Penney and Paul E. Spector, 'Job Stress, Incivility, and Counterproductive Workplace Behavior (CWB): The Moderating Role of Negative Affectivity', *Journal of Organizational Behavior* 26 (2005): 777–96.

9. Daniel P. Skarlicki, Robert Folger and Paul Tesluk, 'Personality as a Moderator Between Fairness and Retaliation' *Academy of Management Journal* 42 (1999): 100–08.

1 Machiavellianism

1. James M. LeBreton, Levi K. Shiverdecker and Elizabeth M. Grimaldi, 'The Dark Triad and Workplace Behavior', *Annual Review of Organizational Psychology and Organizational Behavior* (2017).

2. Ibid.

3. Emily A. Dowgwillo and Aaron L. Pincus, 'Differentiating Dark Triad Traits within and across Interpersonal Circumplex Surfaces', *Journal of Sage Publications* 24(1) (2017): 24–44.

4. Richard P. Bagozzi, William Verbeke, Roeland C. Dietvorst, F.D. Belschak, Wouter E. Van Den Berg and Wim J.R. Rietdijk, 'Theory of Mind and Empathic Explanations of Machiavellianism: A Neuroscience Perspective', *Journal of Management* 39(7) (2013): 1760–98.

5. Elizabeth J. Austin, Daniel Farrelly, Carolyn Black and Helen Moore, 'Emotional Intelligence, Machiavellianism and Emotional Manipulation: Does EI Have a Dark Side?', *Personality and Individual Differences* 43 (2007): 179–89.

2   Narcissism

1. James M. LeBreton, Levi K. Shiverdecker and Elizabeth M. Grimaldi, 'The Dark Triad and Workplace Behavior', *Annual Review of Organizational Psychology and Organizational Behavior* (2017).
2. Aaron L. Pincus, *Initial Construction and Validation of the Pathological Narcissism Inventory* (US Library of Medicine National Institute of Health, 2009), p. 367.
3. Cynthia Mathieu, 'Personality and Job Satisfaction: the Role of Narcissism', *Personality and Individual Differences* 55 (2013): 650–55.
4. Emily A. Dowgwillo and Aaron L. Pincus, 'Differentiating Dark Triad Traits within and across Interpersonal Circumplex Surfaces', *Journal of Sage Publications* 24(1) (2017): 24–44.

3   Psychopathy

1. James M. LeBreton, Levi K. Shiverdecker and Elizabeth M. Grimaldi, 'The Dark Triad and Workplace Behavior', *Annual Review of Organizational Psychology and Organizational Behavior* (2017).
2. Peter Muris, Harald Merckelbach, Henry Otgaar and Ewout Meijer, 'The Malevolent Side of Human Nature: A Meta-Analysis and Critical Review of the Literature on the Dark Triad', *Perspectives on Psychological Science* 12(2) (2017): 183–204.
3. Falkenbach, Poythress, Falki, and Manchak, 2007; Hicks, Markon, Patrick, Krueger, and Newman, 2004; Lykken, 2006
4. Henrik Andershed, Sheilagh Hodgins and Anders Tengström, 'Convergent Validity of the Youth Psychopathic Traits Inventory (YPI) Association with the Psychopathy Checklist: Youth Version (PCL: YV)', *Journal of Sage Publications* 14(2) (2007): 144–54.

5. John F. Rauthmann, 'The Dark Triad and Interpersonal Perception: Similarities and Differences in the Social Consequences of Narcissism, Machiavellianism, and Psychopathy', *Social Psychological and Personality Science,* 3(4) (2012): 487–96.
6. Matt DeLisi, David J. Peters, Tamerria Dansby, Michael G. Vaughn, Jeffrey J. Shook and Andy Hochstetler, 'Dynamics of Psychopathy and Moral Disengagement in the Etiology of Crime', *Youth Violence and Juvenile Justice* 12(4) (2014): 295–314.

4   Neuroticism

1. John Ormel, Harriëtte Riese and Judith G.M. Rosmalen, 'Interpreting Neuroticism Scores across the Adult Life Course: Immutable or Experience-Dependent Set Points of Negative Affect?', *Clinical Psychology Review* 32(1) (2012): 71–79.
2. Paul T. Costa and Robert R. McCrae, 'Domains and Facets: Hierarchical Personality Assessment Using the Revised Neo Personality Inventory', *Journal of Personality Assessment* 64(1) (1995): 21–50.
3. Michael W. Passer and Ronald E. Smith, *Psychology: The Science of Mind and Behaviour* (McGraw-Hill Higher Education, 2009).
4. Kristina De Neve and Harris Cooper, 'The Happy Personality: A Meta-Analysis of 137 Personality Traits and Subjective Well-Being', *Psychological Bulletin* 124 (2) (1998): 197–229.
5. Alec Roy, 'Childhood Trauma and Neuroticism as an Adult: Possible Implication for the Development of the Common Psychiatric Disorders and Suicidal Behaviour', *Psychological Medicine* 32(8) (2002): 1471–74. doi:10.1017/S0033291702006566

5   Everyday Sadists

1. John Reid Meloy, 'The Psychology of Wickedness: Psychopathy and Sadism', *Psychiatric Annals* 27 (1997): 630–33.

2. Vernon J. Gerberth and Ronald N. Turco, 'Antisocial Personality Disorder, Sexual Sadism, Malignant Narcissism, and Serial Murder', *Journal of Forensic Science* 42 (1997): 49–60.
3. Erin E. Buckels, Daniel N. Jones and Delroy L. Paulhus, 'Behavioral Confirmation of Everyday Sadism', *Psychological Science* 24(11) (2013): 2201–09.
4. Aisling O'Meara, Jason Davies and Sean Hammond, 'The Psychometric Properties and Utility of the Short Sadistic Impulse Scale (SSIS)', *Psychological Assessment* 23(2) (2011): 523–31.
5. Delroy L. Paulhus, 'Toward a Taxonomy of Dark Personalities', *Current Directions in Psychological Science 23* (2014): 421–26.

II The Kurus: Personality Assessments of Common Lineage

1 The Dyde: Satyavati And Shantanu

1. Pradip Bhattacharya, 'Of Kunti and Satyawati: Sexually Assertive Women of the Mahabharata', *Manushi* 142 (2004): 21–25.
2. It is believed that Satyavati's fish like smell (Matsygandha) ameliorated to become like deer musk. And with this she got rid of her curse as mentioned before.
3. Ibid.
4. Indrajeet Bandhyopadhyay, *Evolutionary Psychology of Mahabharata* (Calcutta: Lulu Press, Inc., 2013).
5. Kisari Mohan Ganguli, *The Mahabharata of Krishna Dwaipayana Vyasa* (1896).
6. Ibid.
7. Narendra Kohli, *Mahasamar* (1988), p. 83.
8. Dhanalakshmi Ayyer, 'Women of substance: Satyavati: Blind ambition', *The Week* 24(48) (2006): 50.
9. Kisari Mohan Ganguli, *The Mahabharata of Krishna Dwaipayana Vyasa* (1896), p. 209-10.
10. Ibid. p. 210.

11. Kisari Mohan Ganguli, *The Mahabharata of Krishna Dwaipayana Vyasa* (1896).

12. Ibid. p. 218.

13. Robert E. Emery, 'Inter-parental Conflict and the Children of Discord and Divorce', *Psychological Bulletin* 92(2) (1982): 310–30; John H. Grych and Frank D. Fincham, 'Marital Conflict and Children's Adjustment: A Cognitive-Contextual Framework', *Psychological Bulletin* 108 (1990): 267–90; Patrick T. Davies and Mark E. Cummings, 'Marital Conflict and Child Adjustment: An Emotional Security Hypothesis', *Psychological Bulletin* 116 (1994): 387–411; Gordon T. Harold and Rand D. Conger, 'Marital Conflict and Adolescent Distress: The Role of Adolescent Awareness', *Child Development* 68 (1997): 330–50; Philip A. Cowan and Carolyn Pape Cowan, 'Interventions as Tests of Family Systems Theories: Marital and Family Relationships in Children's Development and Psychopathology', *Development and Psychopathology* 14 (2002): 731–59.

14. Charlotte Towle, 'The Evaluation and Management of Marital Status in Foster Homes', *American Journal of Orthopsychiatry* 1 (1931): 271–84.

15. Osnat Erel and Bonnie Burman, 'Interrelatedness of Marital Relationship and Parent-Child Relations: A Meta-Analytic Review', *Psychological Bulletin* 118(1) (1995): 108–32.

16. Ibid.

17. Supra note 1.

18. Mark E. Cummings and Patrick T. Davies, *Marital Conflict and Children: An Emotional Security Perspective* (New York: Guilford, 2010); K. A. Rhoades, 'Children's Responses to Inter-Parental Conflict: A Meta-Analysis of their Associations with Child Adjustment', *Child Development* 79 (2008): 1942–56.

19. Robert E. Emery, 'Inter-parental Conflict and the Children of Discord and Divorce', *Psychological Bulletin* 92(2) (1982): 310–30.

20. Kathleen Camara and Gary Resnick. 'Styles of Conflict Resolution and Cooperation between Divorced Parents: Effects on Child Behavior and Adjustment', *American Journal of Orthopsychiatry* 59(4) (1989): 556–75.

21. *The Tribune* online edition 27.10.2002, www.tribuneindia. com/2002/20021027/herworld.htm#1

22. Carl Gustav Jung, *The Archetypes and the Collective Unconscious* (London: Routledge, 1991), pp. 28–29.

23. Ibid. p. 31.

24. Pradeep Bhattacharya, 'Living by their Own Norms: Unique Powers of the Panchkanyas', *Manushi* 145: 30–37.

25. H. Cederman, 'Women in Mahabharata' (Master of Arts in Religious Studies thesis, University of Canterbury, 1987).

26. Narendra Kohli, *Mahasamar* (1988), p. 53.

27. Ibid. p. 83.

28. Ibid. p. 89.

29. Ibid. p. 111.

30. Ibid.

31. Margarete Vollrath, Franz Neyer, Eivind Ystrom, E. and Markus Landolt, 'Dyadic Personality Effects on Family Functioning in Parents of Newly Hospitalized Children', *Personal Relationships* 17(1) (2010): 27–40.

32. John Sirjamaki, 'Cultural Configurations in the American Family', *American Journal of Sociology* 53 (1948): 464–70.

33. Joan B. Kelly, 'Children's Adjustment in Conflicted Marriage and Divorce: A Decade Review of Research', *Journal of the American Academy of Child & Adolescent Psychiatry* 39(8) (2000): 963–73.

34. Osnat Erel and Bonnie Burman, 'Interrelatedness of Marital Relationship and Parent-Child Relations: A Meta-Analytic Review', *Psychological Bulletin* 118(1) (1995): 108–32.

35. Gordon T. Harold and Rand D. Conger, 'Marital Conflict and Adolescent Distress: The Role of Adolescent Awareness', *Child Development* 68(2) (1997): 333–50.

2 Ambika and Ambalika: The Reluctant Wives and Mothers

1. Sambhava Parva (The Chapter of Possibilities) is the fifth chapter of Book 1. In this chapter, the birth story of Pandu and Dhritarashtra and their marriages are narrated.
2. Kaustav Chakraborty and Rajarshi Guha Thakurata, 'Indian Concepts on Sexuality', *Indian J Psychiatry* 55 (Suppl. 2) (2013): S250–S255.
3. Ibid.

III Kauravas: DNA Preservers

1 The Dyad: Gandhari and Dhritrashtra

1. Praggnaparamita Biswas, 'Interconnectivity of Marriage, Sexuality and Streedharma: Reflections through the Minor Female Characters of the Mahabharata', *Bharatiya Pragna: An Interdisciplinary Journal of Indian Studies* Vol. 1, No. 3 (2016).
2. Dhritarashtra had fourteen sons and one daughter Dusshala, from Gandhari. The names of his sons are: 1) Duryodhana 2) Dushasana 3) Dussaha 4) Dusshala 5) Durdarsha 6) Duspradarshana 7) Durmarshana 8) Durmukha 9) Duskarna 10) Durmada 11) Durvigaha 12) Durvimochana 13) Dusprajya, and 14) Duradhara.

   Dusshala was married to Jayadharata, the king of Sindhu Sauvira. Duryodhana was married to Bhanumati, the princess of Kashi. He had a son and a daughter from her called Lakshman and Lakshamana respectively.

   Dhritarashtra had eighty-seven sons from ten maidservants. The names of four maidservants are known- Vishakha, Sunabhi, Deerghakegi and Vibhavari. The names of their sons are : 1) Yuyutsu 2) Jalsandha 3) Sama 4) Saha 5) Vinda 6) Anuvinda 7) Subhau 8) Karna 9) Vivinsati 10) Vikarna 11) Shull 12) Satva 13) Sulochana 14) Chitra 15) Upchitra 16) Chitraksa 17) Charuchitra 18) Shrasna 19) Vivitsu

20) Viktanana 21) Urnanabha 22) Sunabha 23) Nanda 24) Upnanda 25) Chitrabana 26) Chitravarma 27) Suvarma 28) Ayobahu 29) Mahabahu 30) Chitranga 31) Chitrakundala 32) Bhimvega 33) Bimbala 34) Balaki 35) Balvardhana 36) Ugrayudha 37) Sushena 38) Kundhara 39) Mahodara 40) Chitrayudha 41) Nishangi 42) Pashi 43) Vrndaraka 44) Dradhvarma 45) Dradhksetra 46) Somkirti 47) Anudara 48) Dradhsandha 49) Jarasandha 50) Satyasandha 51) Sadsuvaka 52) Ugrasarva 53) Ugrasena 54) Senani 55) Aprajit 56) Kundshayi 57) Vishalaksa 58) Dradhasta 59) Suhasta 60) Vatvega 61) Suvarcha 62) Adityaketu 63) Bahvashi 64) Nagdatta 65) Agrayayi 66) Kavchi 67) Krthana 68) Kundi 69) Ugra 70) Bhimratha 71) Virbahu 72) Alolupa 73) Abhya 74) Rodarkarma 75) Dradhrathasrya 76) Anadhrasya 77) Kundbhedi 78) Viravi 79) Pramatha 80) Pramathi 81) Dirghroma 82) Dirghabahu 83) Mahabhudhi 84) Yudhoraksa 85) Kanakdhawaja 86) Kundashi, and 87) Virja

[See J.P. Mittal, *History of Ancient India (A New Version) From 4250 BC to 637 AD.* (Atlantic Publishers and Dist., 2006) pp. 465–66] These propositions by the author negates the possibility of Gandhari giving birth to a ball of flesh which was then divided and preserved in 101 pots filled with ghee to produce 100 sons and one daughter as per her boon.

3. Sambhava Parva (The Chapter of Possibilities) is the fifth chapter of Book 1. In this chapter, the birth story of Pandu and Dhritarashtra and their marriages are narrated.

4. In Vyasa's Mahabharata no particular motive is given for the evil mechanism of Shakuni's mind except his physical deformity, and his hatred for order and harmony as a villainous trait for morbidity. But in Sarala's Mahabharata, a fifteenth-century pioneering work in Oriya, Shakuni is given a motive, a cause to uphold, which gloss over his villainy to give him a heroic stature. Duryodhana in his psychic disturbance, at a blind father and a blindfolded mother, had imprisoned the entire royal family of Gandhar, including the king and his hundred children. He used to send one meal a day for the entire family. In a meeting, the Gandhar clan decided

that if they shared the one meal sent to them they would all die in a week or two; they should therefore allow one member of the family to eat that meal and survive to take revenge on Duryodhana. Shakuni was the fateful person selected by the family to survive as the revenge hero. The agony of Shakuni, watching the shriveled death of his entire family in front of his eyes, was suppressed by a simulated grin as a veritable mask. He was intelligent, well-read, good with a sword, and he limped his way across Aryavarta to destroy Duryodhana and the entire Kuru clan. He developed a set of dice with the bones of his dear ones and made it the most potent weapon to manipulate the reality of his times. He entered Duryodhana's household to control the destiny of the heartland of Aryavarta with his crooked pair of dice and became an intellectual, political and strategic counterpoint to the genius of Krishna. [See P.K. Mohanty, 'The "Mahabharata": A Reading in Political Structuring', *Indian Literature–Sahitya Academy*, Vol. 49, No. 1 (225) (2005): 146–51.]

5. Manita Kahlon, 'Women in Mahabharata: Fighting Patriarchy'. https://www.academia.edu/1479293/_Women_in_Mahabharata_Fighting_Patriarchy (accessed December 30, 2017). Web. 532

6. Ibid.

7. The name of the article is 'Mahabharata through the Eyes of Women'.

8. Sons of Pandu, and legal heirs to the throne of Hastinapur (ref. Figure 1).

9. The Adiparva of Mahabharata has references to conflicts about whether the throne should go to the deserving man, or according to genealogical order. Even if an heir is declared on the basis of birth, there are instances of the eldest legitimate son not getting the throne due to lack of physical fitness or the king's decision. The Shatapatha Brahmana does not talk about the regular practice of passing on the throne to the eldest son. 'The genealogical right became entrenched in India because of the varna system.' [See Ram Sharan Sharma,

Aspects of Political Ideas and Institutions in Ancient India (Motilal Banarsidass, 1996).] The concept of hereditary succession and primogeniture became prominent. By the end of the Vedic period, widespread heredity is evident in a ten-generation kingship mentioned in the Shatapatha Brahmana.

10. Swami Rama, *Perennial Psychology of the Bhagavad Gita* (Himalayan Institute Press, 1985), pp. 17-18.
11. Ibid.
12. Ibid.
13. Iravati Karve, *Yuganta–The End of an Epoch* (India: Orient Longman Ltd., 1994), p. 37.
14. Ibid.
15. Ibid, p. 38.
16. Ibid.
17. Krishna Chaitanya, *The Mahabharata: A Literary Study* (New York: Clarion Books, 1985).

2   Duryodhana: A Judgemental Assessment

1.   Ronald J. Deluga, 'Relationship among American Presidential Charismatic Leadership, Narcissism, and Rated Performance', *The Leadership Quarterly* 8(1) (1997): 49–65.
2.   Arijit Chatterjee and Donald C. Hambrick, 'It's All About Me: Narcissistic Chief Executive Officers and Their Effects on Company Strategy and Performance', *Administrative Science Quarterly* 52(3) (2007): 351–86.
3.   Duryodhana is generally identified with evil, right from his birth. The Mahabharata describes his birth as bringing in evil portents which spell doom for the Kuru clan and the elders advising Dhritarashtra and Gandhari to abandon this wanton child for the benefit of their race. The wise Vidura says, 'O King, O bull among men, when these frightful omens are noticeable at the birth of thy eldest son, it is evident that he shall be the exterminator of thy race.' [See Adi Parva, Section CXV, Page 242.] The parents understandably ignore the advice and dote on their firstborn and the seeds of Duryodhana's obstinate

character are sown there. He grows up into a fine young boy, but along with him grows his jealousy for the Pandavas.
4. Sabha Parva, Section LIV, p. 109.
5. Adi Parva, Section CXXVIII, p. 267
6. Historiometry is the historical study of human progress or individual personal characteristics, using statistical analysis.
7. Adi Parva, Section CXXVIII, p. 267.
8. Narendra Kohli, *Mahasamar Part 6* (1988), p. 169.
9. Narendra Kohli, *Mahasamar Part 6* (1988), p. 355.
10. Vana Parva, Section CCXXXVI, p. 481.
11. Narendra Kohli, *Mahasamar Part 6* (1988), p. 106.
12. Narendra Kohli, *Mahasamar Part 6* (1988), p. 107.
13. Kisari Mohan Ganguli, *The Mahabharata of Krishna Dwaipayana Vyasa–Vana Parva*, 363–1 (1896).
14. Narendra Kohli, *Mahasamar Part 6* (1988), p. 260.
15. Ibid.
16. Narendra Kohli, *Mahasamar Part 6* (1988), p. 266.
17. Narendra Kohli, *Mahasamar Part 7* (1988), pp. 148–49.
18. Narendra Kohli, *Mahasamar Part 7* (1988), p. 156.
19. There are many other such instances that are indicative of Duryodhana's personality; I am limiting the description in order to avoid repetitions and redundancies. As per historiometry, researchers need to describe only as many number of events from the subject's life as are sufficient to draw dispositional conclusions.

IV Pandavas: Positive Counterparts

1 Pandu: A Brief and Uninfluential Life

1. [NOTE MISSING]
2. Individuals with higher levels of narcissism are likely to (a) harbour feelings of superiority driven by an inflated or grandiose sense of self, (b) have a dysfunctional need for excessive attention and admiration, (c) have a propensity for engaging in exploitative acts or behaviours, and (d) lack

empathy, tending toward callousness. (Morf and Rhodewalt, 2001; Paulhus and Williams, 2002; Raskin and Hall, 1979; Raskin and Terry, 1988; Rhodewalt and Morf, 1995; Wright et al., 2013; Wu and LeBreton, 2011).

3. Quinta Gomes and Pedro Nobre, 'Personality Traits and Psychopathology on Male Sexual Dysfunction: An Empirical Study', *The Journal of Sexual Medicine* 8(2) (2011): 461–69. https://www.ncbi.nlm.nih.gov/pubmed/21054796

4. Refer to the document [document or section in this book?] analyzing the personalities of Ambika and Ambalika for details.

2   Kunti: An Inconsistent DNA to Pandavas

1. C. Rajagopalachari, *Mahabharata* (New Delhi: Bharatiya Vidya Bhavan, 2009).

2. Krishna Chaitanya, *The Mahabharata: A Literary Study* (New York: Clarion Books, 1985).

3. C. Rajagopalachari, *Mahabharata* (New Delhi: Bharatiya Vidya Bhavan, 2009).

4. Iravati Karve, *Yuganta—The End of an Epoch* (India: Orient Longman Ltd., 1994).

5. Kunti's father was a Yadava prince called Shurasena. He had a very dear friend and cousin called Kuntibhoja. This friend was childless. It was customary in those times for heirless kings to seek the favour and blessings of a Brahmin in order to get a son. The chosen Brahmin would be a guest in the palace, fed and waited upon by the daughter of the house. Since Kuntibhoja didn't even have a daughter, he asked his friend Shurasena for Kunti as a gift, and Shurasena gave her away. Kunti's own name was Pritha. It shows that she was apparently a large, big-boned girl. She was better known as Kunti, which means 'a princess of the kingdom of Kunti'.

6. The Udyoga Parva or the Book of Effort, is the fifth of eighteen books of the Mahabharata.

3 Pandavas: Evil Actions and Connivances

1. Juarez (2014)
2. Kisari Mohan Ganguli, *The Mahabharata of Krishna Dwaipayana Vyasa–Adi Parva*, Section CLXIV, p. 334.
3. 'As the ravishing beauty of Panchali who had been modeled by the Creator himself, was superior to that all other women on earth . . .', the Pandavas looked at Draupadi, and '. . . the God of Desire invaded their hearts and continued to crush all their senses.' [See Adi Parva, Section CLXLIII, p. 381].
4. Kisari Mohan Ganguli, *The Mahabharata of Krishna Dwaipayana Vyasa–Udyoga Parva*, Section XVIII, p. 31.
5. Kisari Mohan Ganguli, *The Mahabharata of Krishna Dwaipayana Vyasa–Adi Parva*, Section CXXXIX, p. 290.
6. Vana Parva, Section CCLXX, p. 528.
7. Kisari Mohan Ganguli, *The Mahabharata of Krishna Dwaipayana Vyasa–Adi Parva*, Section CXXXIV, p. 281.
8. An *akshauhini* is described in the Mahabharata as a battle formation consisting of 21,870 chariots, 21,870 elephants, 65,610 horses and 1,09,350 infantries (as per the Mahabharata Adi Parva 2.15-23).

4 Draupadi: A Critical Catalyst to Duryodhanization

1. Sabha Parva.
2. The Mahabharata, Book 2: Sabha Parva: Sisupala-badha Parva: Section XLVI.
3. The Mahabharata, Book 2: Sabha Parva: Sisupala-badha Parva: Section LXVI.
4. The Mahabharata, Book 2: Sabha Parva: 67:42.
5. Ibid.
6. Vana Parva, 10.127.
7. Udyoga Parva, 82.45, 48.
8. Vana Parva, 10.125.

V Some Vague Inductive Reasoning and Generalizations

1. Romila Thapar, *A History of India*.
2. Q.C. Rufus, *The History of Alexander* (London: Penguin Books, 2005).
3. S.A.A. Rizvi, *The Wonder that was India Vol. 2* (London: Sidgwick and Jackson, 1987).
4. Sri Ram Sharma, *The Religious Policy of Mughal Emperors* (London: Asia Publ. House, 1962).
5. Annemarie Schimmel, *The Empire of the Great Mughals* Opcit., p. 145.
6. J.N. Chaudhary, 'Mumtaz Mahal', *Islamic Culture* (1937): 373.
7. Fergus Nicoll, *Shah Jahan* (India: Penguin Books, 2009).
8. John F. Richards, *NCHI: The Mughal Empire* (Cambridge: Cambridge University Press 1993); Neeru Misra, *Succession and Imperial Leadership among the Mughals 1526–1707* (New Delhi: Konark Publishers, 1993).
9. Zahiruddin Faruki, *Aurangzeb and His Times* (Bombay: Taraporevala Sons and Co., 1935).
10. Athar M. Ali, *The Mughal Nobility under Aurangzeb* (London: Asia Publishing House, 1968).
11. Robert C. Hallissey, *The Rajput Rebellion Against Aurangzeb* (Missouri-Columbia University Press, 1977).
12. Supra note 2.
13. Catherine B. Asher, *Aurangzeb and the Islamization of the Mughal style in New Cambridge History of India (NCHI): Mughal Architecture in India* (Cambridge: Cambridge University Press, 1992) pp. 252–91.
14. W. Crooke, *The Northwestern Provinces of India* (New Delhi: Oxford University Press, 1992 Reprint).
15. For a summary of the detailed report, see http://www.lawschool.cornell.edu/library/whatwehave/specialcollections/donovan/hitler/upload/vol_xc_sec_1.pdf
16. Ibid.

17. See Alfred Adler, *The Individual Psychology of Alfred Adler*, eds. H.L. Ansbacher and R.R. Ansbacher (New York: Harper Torchbooks, 1956).; R. Lehrer, 'Adler and Nietzsche'. In: J. Golomb, W. Santaniello, and R. Lehrer. (Eds.). Nietzsche and Depth Psychology. (Albany, NY: State University of New York Press, 1999), pp. 229–46. Hertha Orgler, *Alfred Adler: The Man and His Work: Triumph Over the Inferiority Complex* (New York: Liveright, 1963). [http://journalpsyche.org/alfred-adler-personality-theory/]

18. Ibid.

19. Rainer Funk, *Erich Fromm: His Life and Ideas–An Illustrated Biography* (New York: Continuum, 2000).

20. Ileen Bear, *Adolf Hitler: A Biography* (Vij Books India Pvt. Ltd., 2016).

21. Brigitte Hamann, *Hitler's Vienna* (New York: Tauris Parke Paperbacks, 2010) pp. 10–11.

22. Fritz Redlich, *Hitler: Diagnosis of a Destructive Prophet* (New York: Oxford University Press, 1998) p. 448. illustrated.

23. August Kubizek, *The Young Hitler I Knew: The Memoirs of Hitler's Childhood Friend* (1955).

24. Ibid.

25. Supra note 8.

Conclusion

1. A story inspired by the work of Jayant Khatri–*Khoon ki Boond* (Drop of Blood), Lokbharti Prakashan, Delhi.

2. HARKing is defined as presenting a post-hoc hypothesis (i.e. one based on or informed by one's results) in one's research report as if it were, in fact, an a priori hypotheses. Several forms of HARKing are identified and survey data presented, that suggests that at least some forms of HARKing are widely practiced, and widely seen as inappropriate (Kerr, 1998).